Excel In A Snap

Excel In A Snap

Learn Excel Basics In A Single Weekend

By Crystal Allen

Printed in the United States of America.

ISBN: **979-8-2850779-5-4**

www.INaSnapGuides.com

First Edition

In loving memory of my brother, Richard Scott McKinnis, the fire department captain and hazardous materials specialist who once told me, "The one tutorial I need is for Excel."

Table of Contents

Table of Contents

Table of Contents

Introduction

This book is for people who don't have five months to learn Excel. Not even five weeks. This is for the person who needs to master the basics of Excel in a single weekend before they start their new job. Or that college student who's already slammed and just wants to learn Excel in, you know, a snap!

Excel In A Snap can make you Excel proficient in a single weekend. There are 8 projects and 78 exercises in this tutorial. Also included are over 200 screenshots, most of them illustrated with circles, arrows, and text boxes to clarify the click path, which is essential to mastering any software.

Together these projects and exercises encompass a broad scope including formatting cells and headers, sorting and filtering data, adding and removing rows and columns, freezing rows and columns, hiding rows and columns, mathematical formulas for real-life financial scenarios, an easily updateable mortgage amortization table that you will make yourself; bar charts, pie charts, line graphs, collapsible lists, and a bonus section devoted to Pivot Tables and VLookup.

Here's some good news. Most software experts agree that 20% of any given software application is used for roughly 80-90% of tasks a worker would typically perform with that software tool in an office environment.

This tutorial will teach you that 20 percent of Excel functionality you can use for up to 90 percent of your on-the-job Excel tasks.

So, what about the other 10-20 percent? Well, once you have mastered the 20 percent that covers the 90 percent, it's fairly easy to fine-tune your expertise. You can easily search for that specific information based on what you already know about Excel or just click around in the app and figure it out yourself.

I learned Excel on the job. I'll show you how the Excel formula bar works right up front because I could not do a thing with Excel until I knew that. Everything else that you will find in this blissfully short book I learned on my own.

Every bit of Excel functionality that I have used on the job as a communications and project manager for a Fortune 500 software company is in this book. Short, sweet, and to the point.

While it takes most people roughly 16-20 hours to run through the exercises and projects up to the bonus section, it can take some people more time than others. Many folks can do it in 8 hours or less.

The bonus section on Pivot Tables and the VLookup tool may take some students another 8 hours and others another weekend. Keep in mind Pivot Tables and VLookup are considered intermediate to advanced-level Excel. Mastering these skills is enough to distinguish you as a go-to Excel person in most office environments.

Before we get started, I'd like to explain the layout of this book. I have written it in two different fonts—Cambria and Ariel bold. I did this to separate the instructions you need to follow from the narrative describing the purpose behind the instructions. That makes it easier to follow directions—one more way to speed things up.

Some readers might find the following material repetitive, possibly redundant. That's because I'd rather provide material in a format that readers can skip if they like, as opposed to forcing some readers to turn back the pages in search of prior instructions, which again wastes time.

This guide covers Excel as part of Office 365 for Mac and Windows. While Excel continues to evolve with new features, the basics will likely never change, which is what this guide covers. What you learn here will serve you for years to come. Only Excel for Mac and Windows computers is covered here. Excel for tablets and smart phones is beyond the scope of this book, although many of the features are the same.

While the basic click-path for most Excel functions remains unchanged from one update to the next, the appearance of the Excel interface, including the appearance of symbols and worksheets can change noticeably. Many of the screenshots in this book are from older versions while most of them are from the latest version of Excel. I felt it was important for my readers to understand that various versions of an application can have different appearances even as the overall functionality remains the same. This can help those of you who need to make the transition from a home laptop to a work laptop.

Here's a final word for PC users. This tutorial was written on a Mac where most of the screenshots were taken. However, there are alternative PC screenshots for PC users when necessary. Also, please keep in mind that anytime this tutorial mentions the Command key (□), that is the equivalent of the Control key on the PC. In regard to the Mac and PC keyboard, the Return key on the Mac is the same as the Enter key on the PC.

Let's dive in.

Opening the Excel App

Your computer might have an Excel quick launch icon on your task bar or application dock. Look for the Excel logo at the bottom of your screen. Double-click it to open the application.

If you don't see it in the dock, you'll need to look for it in the Mac Applications folder or Windows Start menu.

Excel Logo

On a Mac, look for the Finder icon in your dock to the far left (at the bottom of your desktop screen). The Mac's Finder icon is a line-drawn face that is half blue and half white.

The Windows 11 Start Menu icon is a multi-paned "window" as shown below on the right. The Start Menu for older Windows versions may have a different design.

Ma

Launching Excel For Mac

1. **Click on the Finder icon to open a Finder window.**
2. **On the left Sidebar, select Applications.**
3. **In the Content pane look under 'M' for Microsoft Excel.**
4. **If you don't see that, you will likely see a folder labeled Microsoft Office Suite. Click that to find the Excel application.**
5. **Double-click to open it.**

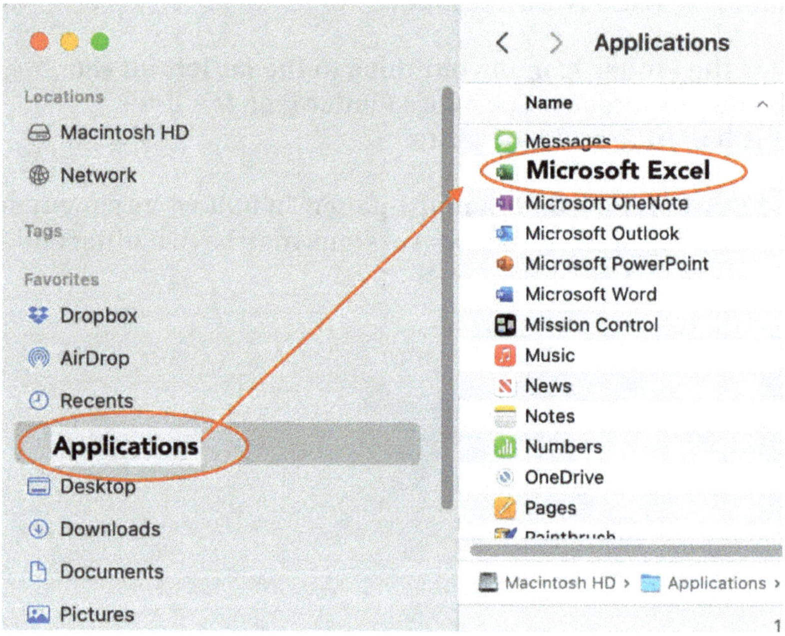

Keeping Excel in Your Dock For Mac

Putting an Excel quick launch icon on your dock can give you easy access to the application. To do this:

1. Click on the Microsoft Excel App to select it.
2. Then click-and-hold while you drag it down to the dock and release it.

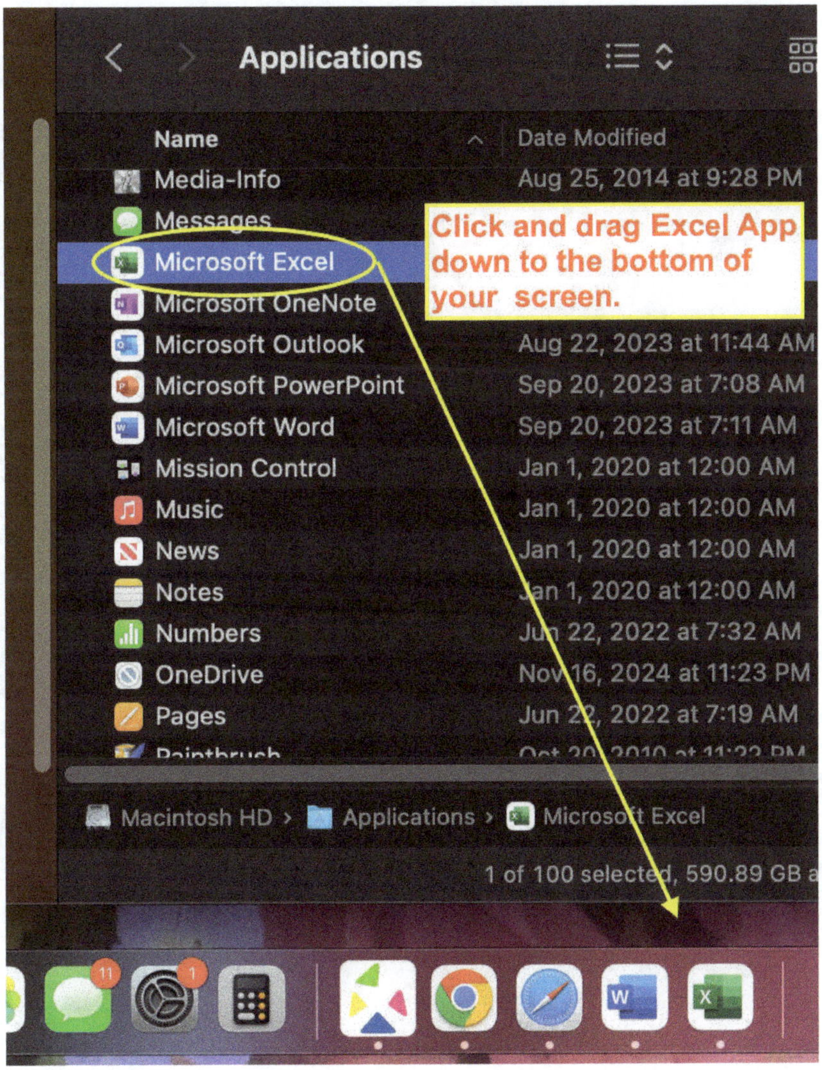

Launching Excel For Windows

1. **Click on the Start Menu Icon to open Start Menu.**
2. **If Excel is pinned in the Start Menu, click its icon.**

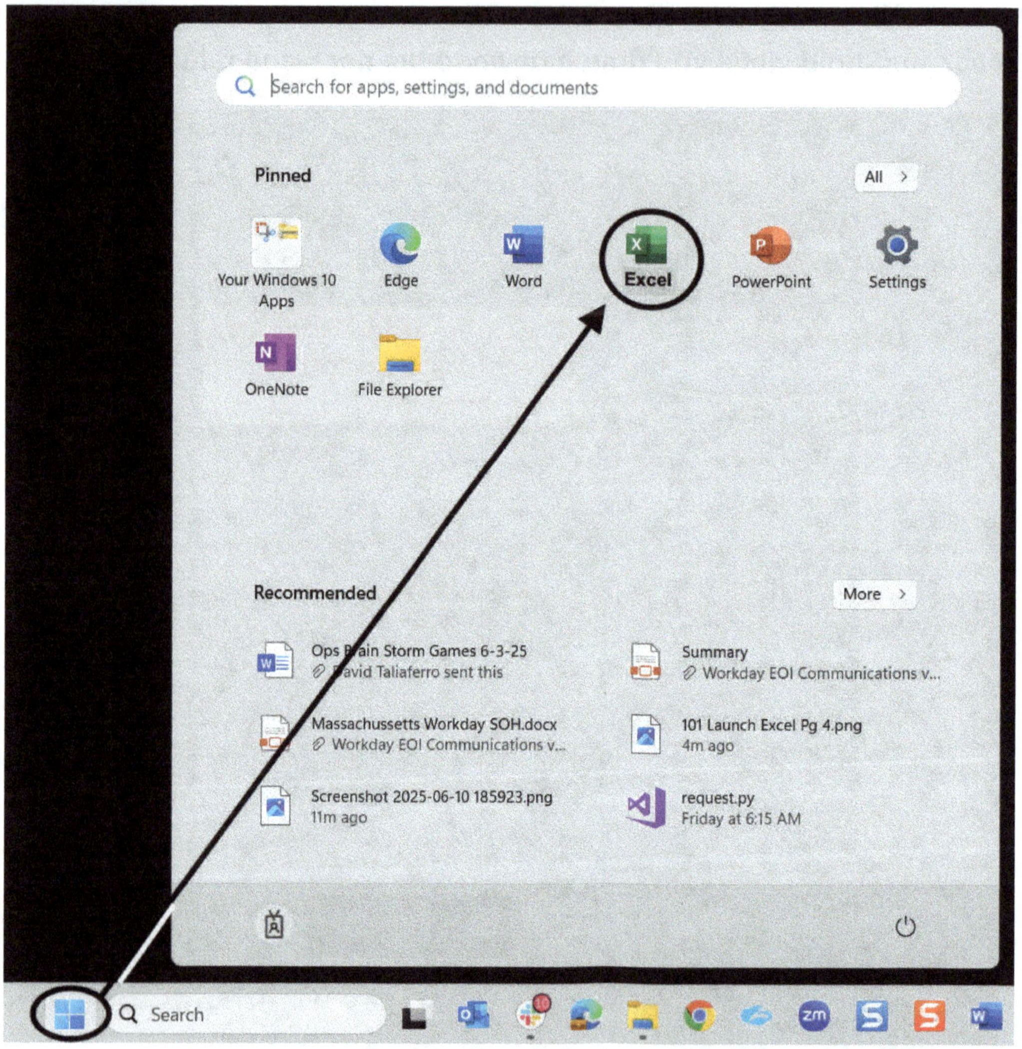

3. If not, click All to expand the applications menu.
4. Look under E, and then click on Excel to open it.

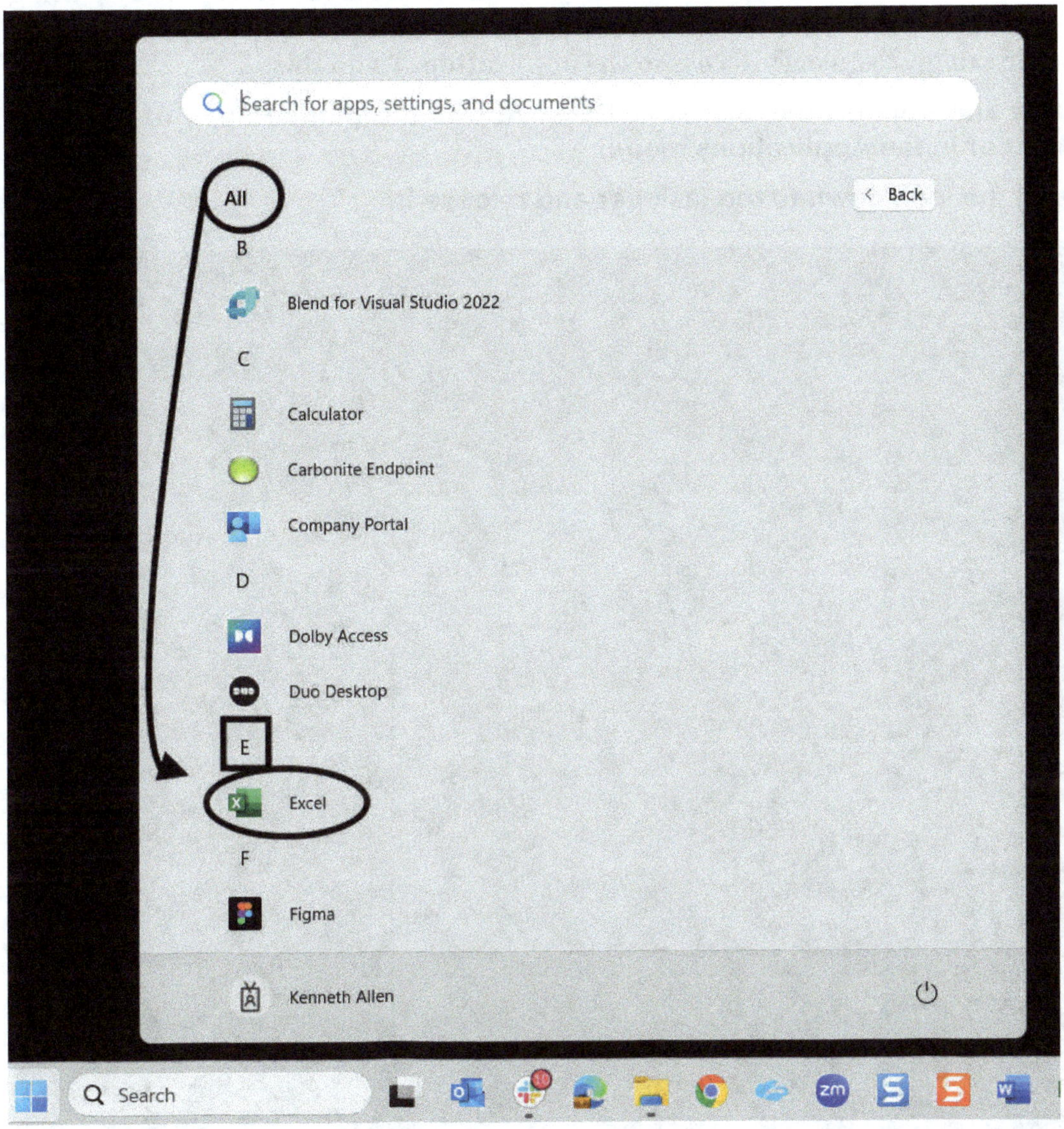

Pinning Excel in Your Task Bar for Windows

"Pinning" refers to making an application, file, or folder icon readily accessible by placing it on the taskbar or start menu for quick access. **Pinning an Excel quick launch icon on your taskbar can give you easy access to the application. To do this:**

1. **Click and hold on the Microsoft Excel App in the pinned apps of the Start Menu or in the Applications menu.**
2. **Drag the icon down to the task bar and release it.**

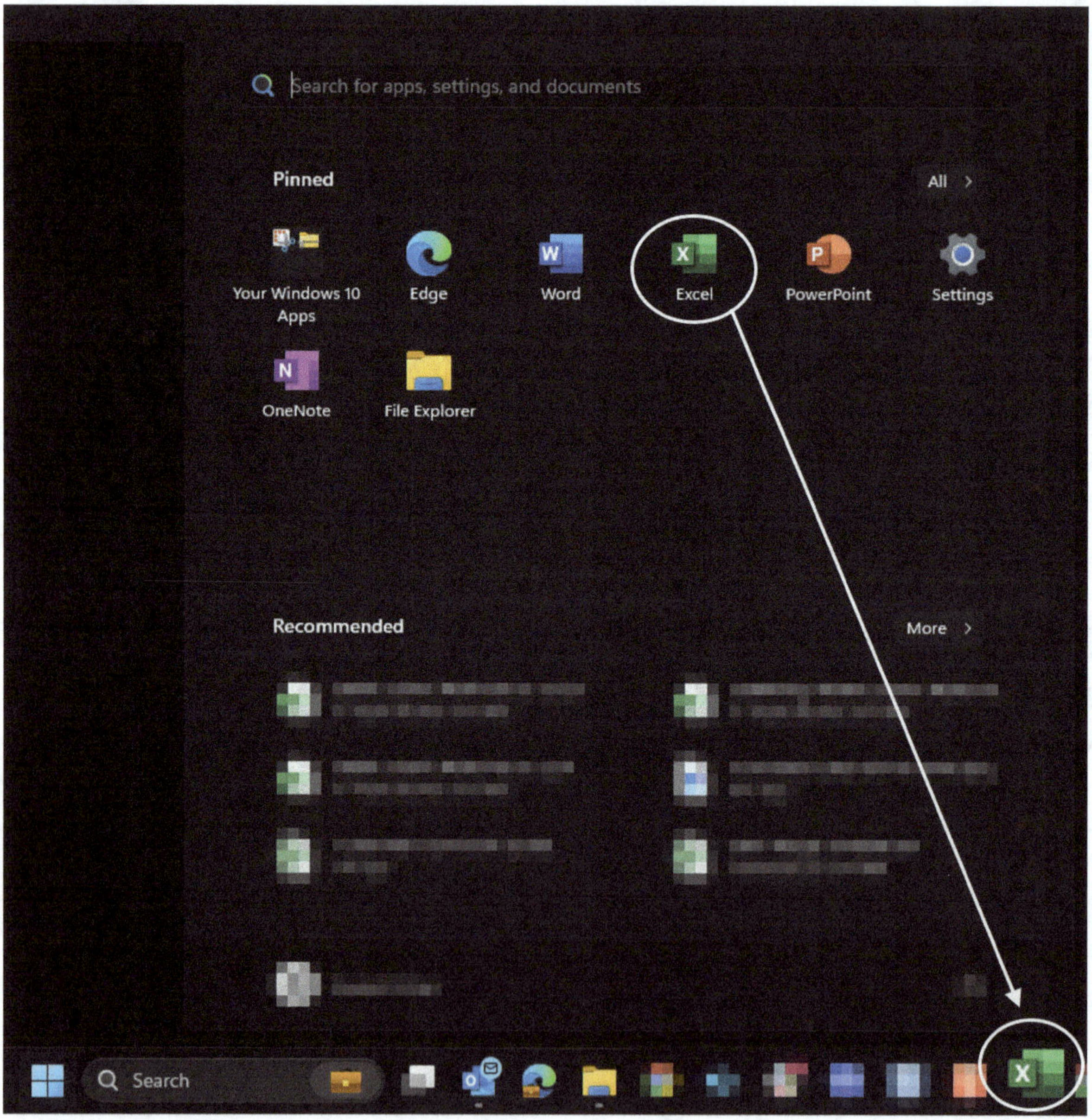

The Basics of the Excel Interface

1. Excel for Mac

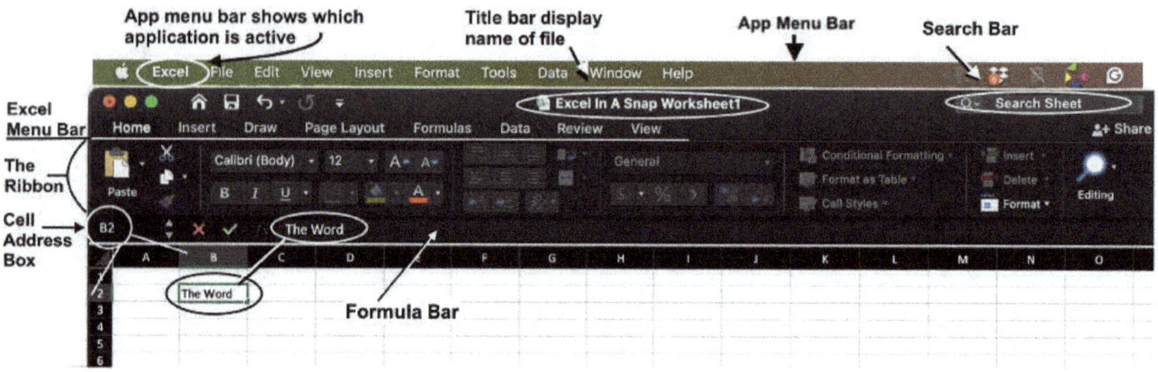

2. Excel for Windows

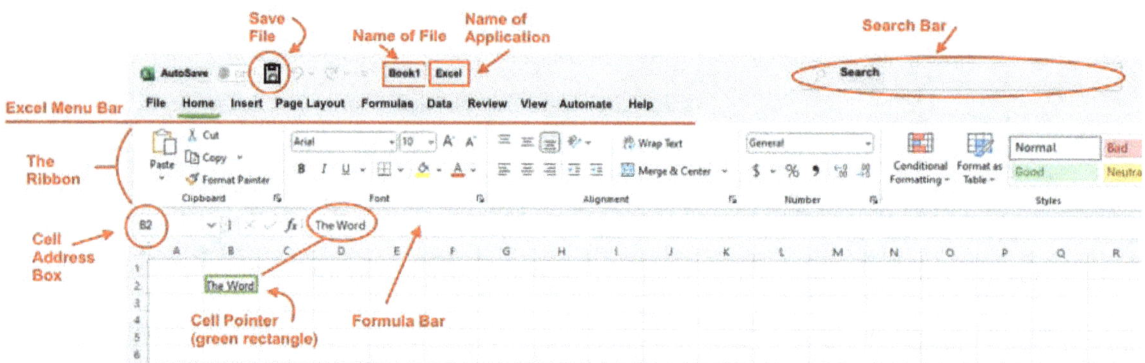

3. Excel 365 Online

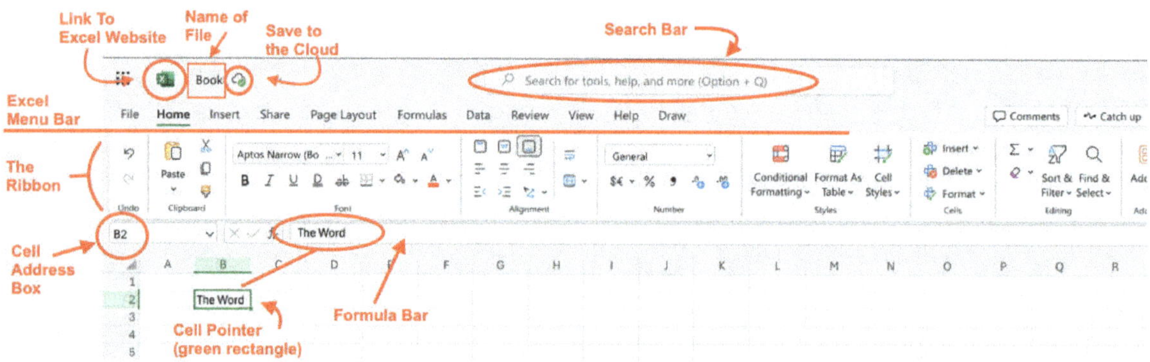

The three screenshots on the previous page illustrate the interface for 1. Excel For Mac,

2. Excel For Windows, and 3. Excel 365 Online. These are the most common Excel interfaces.

If you have a Mac, look at the very top of your computer screen for a thin, gray, horizontal banner. This is the *App Menu Bar.* When you click on a tab on the App Menu Bar, such as File or Format a cascading pop-up toolbox will appear. The App Menu Bar is specific to the Mac personal computer, although the tabs listed horizontally on the App Menu Bar can change depending on the software application that is currently active. PCs don't have an App Menu Bar, all of the tools are found on the Excel Menu Bar, and the Ribbon.

Notice the word 'Excel' at the far left of the App Menu Bar. This means the Excel app is active, i.e., you have placed your pointer in the Excel program and clicked to select it. The App Menu Bar will update when another application is active. For instance, 'Word' will appear if you are editing a Word file.

Beneath the App Menu Bar is the Excel window. You will find the name of the file at the top-center of the window, in this case "Excel In A Snap Worksheet1.xlsx"

The Toolbars and Basic Functions

The *Excel Menu Bar* is near the top on all three interfaces. On the Mac, the Excel Menu Bar is the line of tabs that read Home, Insert, Draw, Page Layout, Formulas, Data, Review, View. The other two interfaces have Excel Menu Bars that begin with "File, Home, Insert..." All three are somewhat different, but they all appear in the same area of the interface.

When you select any one of those tabs, the dashboard of application tools that appears beneath that tab is known as *the ribbon*. The app tools on the ribbon will change each time you click a tab on the Excel Menu Bar.

Tip: If you are searching for a specific tool and can't find it, check to see which menu bar tab you are on.

It's not uncommon to lose track of where you are on these complex toolbars within toolbars. If you need to find a specific word or formula, use the search bar found at the top right of the interface to type it in. For example, if you type in the formula =SUM(B2*B8) in the search bar, the cell pointer will consecutively highlight any or all cells that contain that formula, even though you cannot see it in the cell. If you search for a word or number, those will be shown in the selected cells.

In all three interfaces, the Cell Pointer is the rectangle (usually green or blue) around the selected cell, in this case B2. This color can vary depending on the version of Excel you are using.

Look at the Cell Address Box, (aka Cell Name Box) on the far left. The alphanumeric 'B2' is displayed, because the cell B2 is selected.

Notice the Formula Bar directly to the right of the Cell Address Box. Whereas the Cell Address Box displays the *location* **of the selected cell, the Formula Bar displays the** *content* **of the selected cell.**

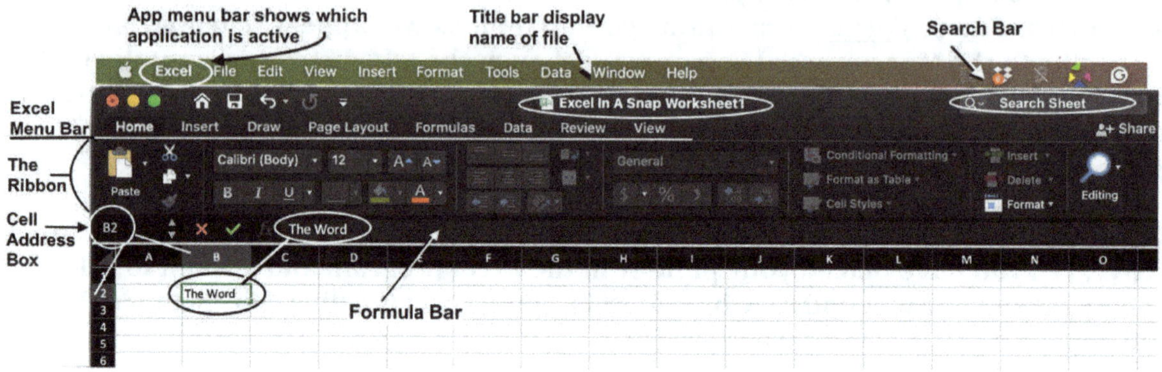

The Formula Bar contains the text 'The Word' because that is the content of the selected cell. If the cell contained a mathematical formula, you would see a number in the cell, but the Formula Bar would contain the mathematical formula that produced that number. We'll explore that more in the section on formulas.

Once you have typed or pasted information into a cell and hit Return on Mac or Enter on Windows, you *cannot* **select that cell and edit it without overwriting the original content.**

To edit content in a cell, you must select the cell, then click on the Formula Bar and make the changes there. Or you can double-click on the cell and make edits without overwriting the original contents.

The following section covers basic functions you can use to create or update any Excel worksheet. Some of these functions you may recognize from other popular software, but many are specific to Excel.

Tip: Every Excel file is a workbook and each sheet is a worksheet.

Name and Save Your Excel Workbook on a Mac

One easy mistake is working on a workbook without first saving it to a specific location. Many documents get lost that way.

If you've just opened a new Excel workbook, at the very top and center you should see the word 'Book1'. That is the default name of every Excel workbook. To save it with a name of your choice:

1. Be sure your Excel application is selected (click anywhere on the worksheet to select).
2. For a Mac: On the App Menu Bar, click FileàSave As.

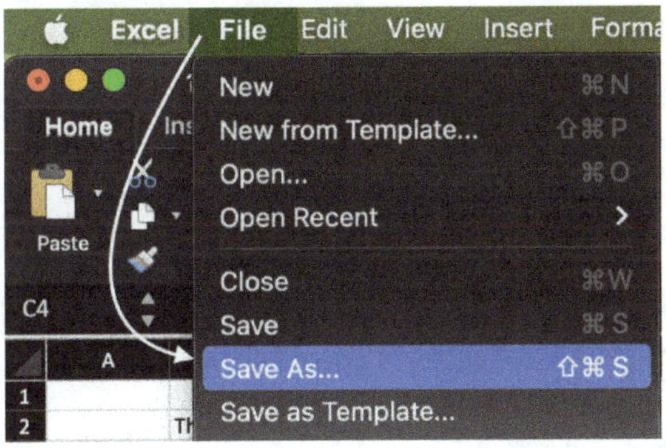

In the pop-up window that appears, the default name of the file (top center) will be selected (see screenshot below).

3. Change the default name to 'Excel In A Snap Worksheet1" or a similar name.
4. On the left side bar choose a file location (usually Documents or Desktop).
5. You can either hit Save at that point or you can choose a folder and then save.

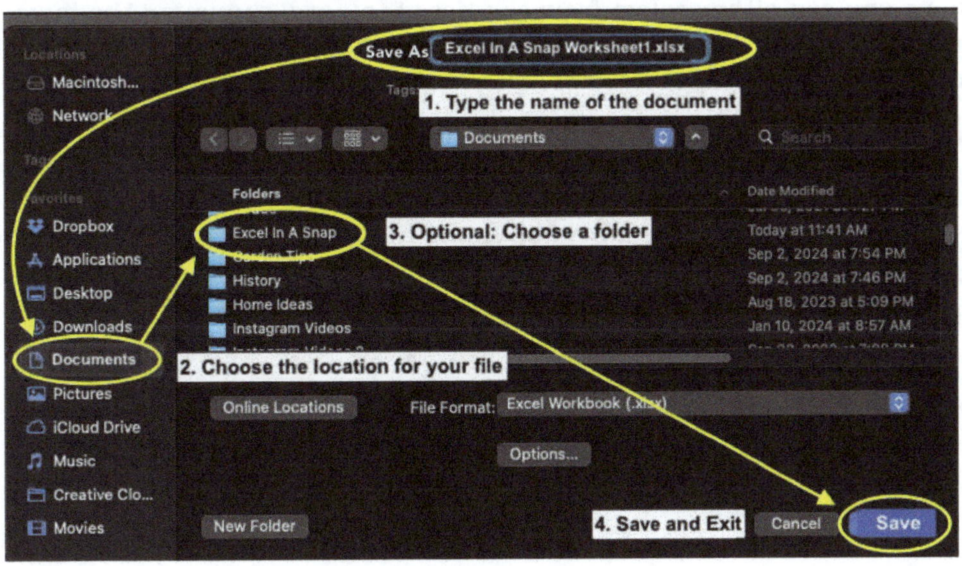

Name and Save Your Excel Workbook on Windows

1. Click File in the Excel menu to the left of the Home tab or click the floppy disc symbol in the Quick Access menu.
2. In the pop-up window, look at the menu bar on the left and click Save As and then This PC (see below).

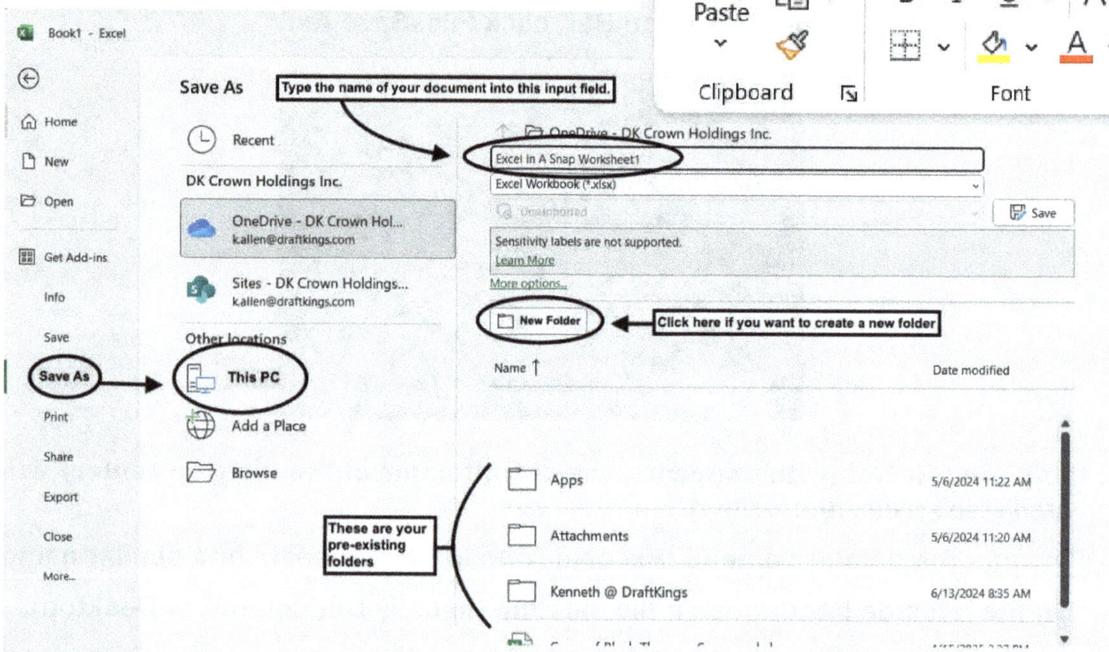

From there you can either select from the list of folders, shown on the lower right of the screenshot, or you can click the New Folder tab directly above. Or you could save your Excel document without a folder.

3. In the top text field, type in the name of the file 'Excel In A Snap Worksheet1' as shown in the oval in the upper right.

If you're saving to a folder, the label above the filename field will be the name of that folder.

4. Click Save on the bottom right of the screen.

Expand Your Excel Window

1. **Hover your pointer over the right edge of your Excel window.**

Your pointer will change to a double-horizontal arrow (see below).

2. **Click and drag to the right to expand the screen horizontally. (*To click-and-drag, press your index finger on the left mouse button and hold down while you move your mouse.)***

Expanding your Excel window horizontally doesn't just make it bigger; it can reveal hidden tools on your toolbars. If you cannot find certain tools, it's best to maximize the width of your Excel window.

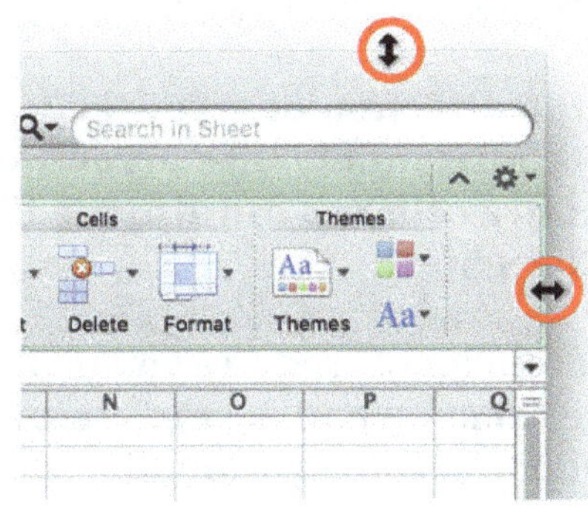

You can also expand your Excel window vertically by hovering your pointer over the upper or lower edge. This function works on most software programs.

You can expand or contract your Excel window and maintain the proportions if you do it from the lower right corner.

1. **Hover your pointer over the corner until it turns into a diagonal double-arrow.**
2. **Click and drag.**

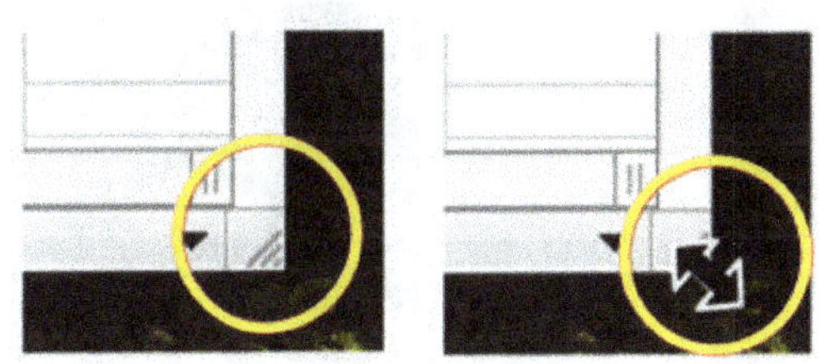

Scrolling

Scrolling functions can vary among different models of touch pads and mouses. It's a good idea to practice the scrolling feature on your worksheet.

Select cell A1 by placing the pointer over the cell and clicking.

Most mouses have a wheel in the center that you move up and down with your index finger to scroll vertically.

Use the direction or arrow keys (on keyboard, lower right, four keys with arrows) to scroll horizontally. Use arrows when you are trying to place the cursor at a certain point in a cell. You can also use the arrow keys to move the cell pointer up or down, or left to right.

Most touchpads require you to place your index and middle fingertips side-by-side and move them up and down to scroll. In Excel, you can also move your index fingers side-to-side to scroll horizontally.

Observe the changes in the column headings and row headings as you scroll. If you get lost in the woods, you can use the Cell Address Box to find your way back. Just type in A1.

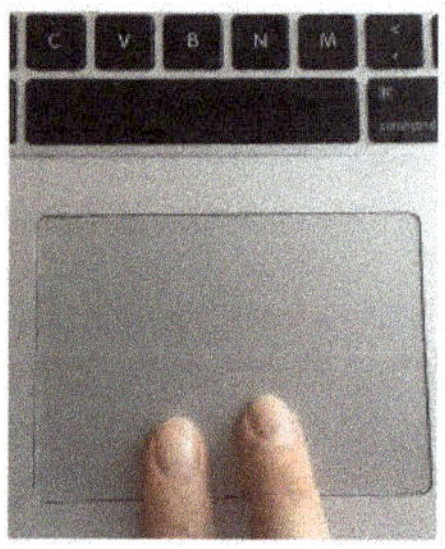

Excel Worksheet Tabs

Every Excel file has the capacity for multiple sheets which you can create at your convenience.

To name your current worksheet:

1. **Go to the bottom of the active Excel window.**
2. **Find the tab that says Sheet1.**
3. **Place your pointer over the Sheet1 tab; double-click to select.**
4. **Type "Worksheet1".**

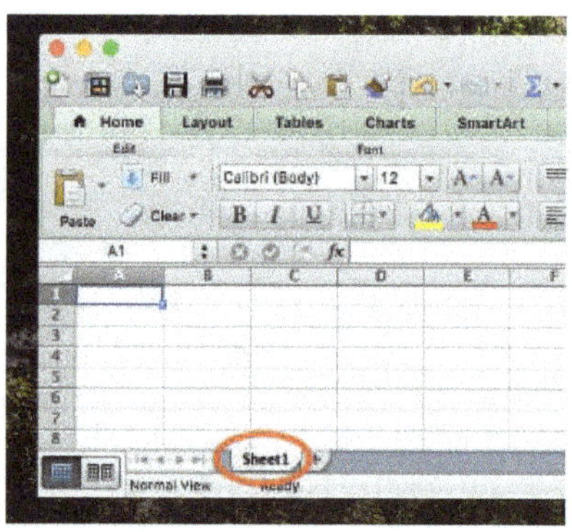

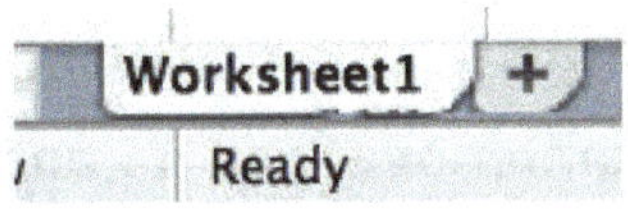

Notice to the right of the *Worksheet1* tab is a smaller tab with a plus-sign.

5. Click on the tab to open a new worksheet.

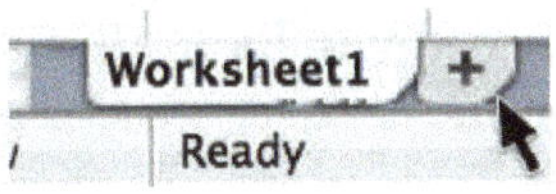

The name of the new tab defaults to Sheet2. The plus-sign tab next to the Sheet2 tab indicates you can open a large number of sheets, up to 255 in total. Click back to *Worksheet1*.

For later exercises you can go to our website—INaSnapGuides.com—to download the *Excel In A Snap Worksheets* file. This file contains a total of 12 worksheets that will give you a head start on the eight projects included in the tutorial. If you cannot download the workbook, you can easily fill in your own with the information provided in this guide.

In either case, you will soon be managing numerous Excel worksheets, each with a tab of its own at the bottom of the Excel window.

If you have more tabs than can be displayed, navigate those tabs by clicking the triangular arrows on the far left of the tab bar as shown below. Click the right arrow to scroll right and the left arrow to scroll left.

Cell Address Box and Cell Pointer

1. Place your pointer over cell A1 and click to select.
2. Move your pointer to the Cell Address Box (upper left) and click to select.
3. Type 'B2' and hit Return for Mac or Enter for Windows.

Notice the cell pointer jumps to cell B2. The Cell Address Box (or Cell Name Box) can be used to select a specific cell in a large, complicated worksheet, or to determine at a glance which column and row your cell pointer is in.

You can also determine the exact location of your cell pointer by observing the darkened row and column headings.

Notice when the cell pointer is in cell B2, the row number '2' and column header 'B' are both darkened. (If your computer is set to dark mode, they are a lighter shade.)

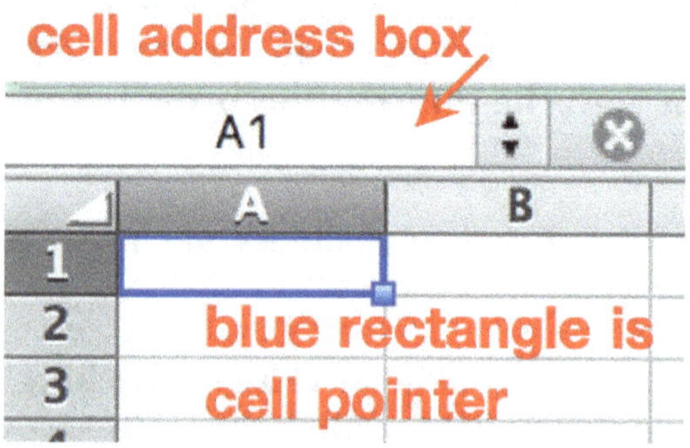

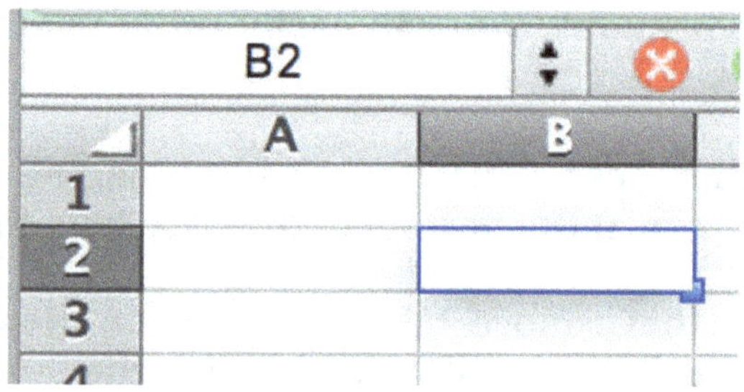

Formula Bar and Cell Content

1. Place your curser in cell A1, type "the cat".
2. Hit Return/Enter.

Notice the cell pointer automatically moves to cell A2. If you want to advance horizontally to B1, hit the tab button on your keyboard.

3. Move your pointer to A1, click to select, and type "is outstanding" and hit Return on Mac or Enter on Windows.

Notice the original text disappears and is overwritten by the new text.

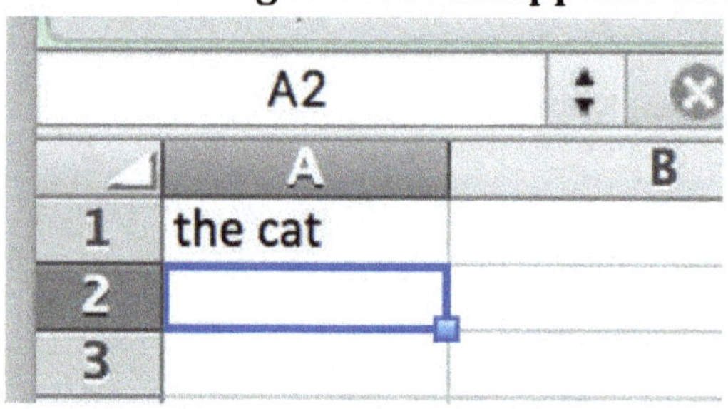

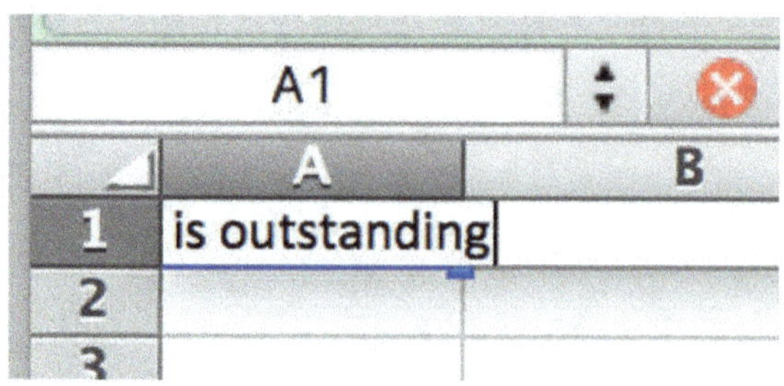

To update the contents of a cell without overwriting it, you must make updates in the Formula Bar.

4. **Select A1. Type "the cat" and hit Return/Enter.**
5. **Click back into cell A1.**

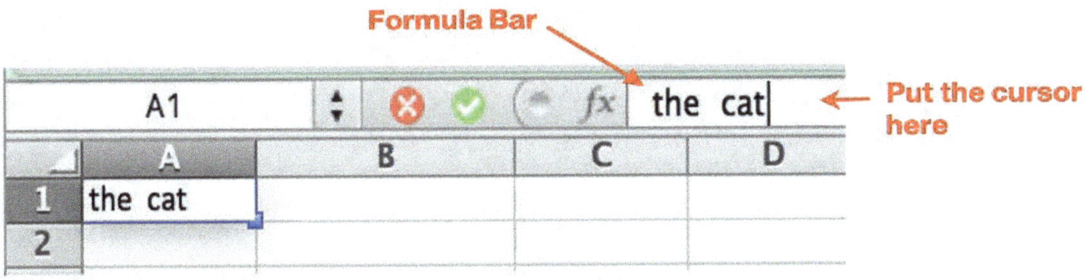

6. **Move the pointer to the Formula Bar.**
7. **Place the pointer at the end of the word "cat" and click to select.**
8. **Type "is outstanding".**
9. **Hit Return on Mac or Enter on Windows.**

Notice the phrase "the cat is outstanding" spills over into cell B2

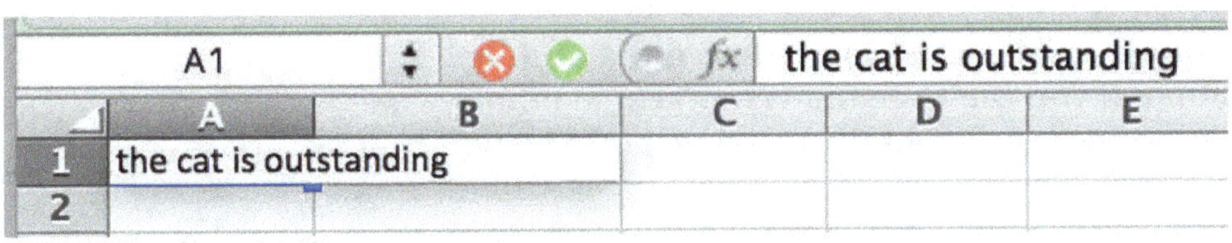

Tip: If you want to update the content without going to the Formula Bar, double-click the cell and you can make changes without overwriting the original content.

Cell Formatting Basics

Mastering cell formatting techniques can give you a lot of control over the appearance of your spreadsheets.

The following exercises don't cover all formatting possibilities, but we'll explore the most common cases to create a professional spreadsheet. This is also a good opportunity to apply corporate colors and type fonts to your work.

In the exercise on the preceding page, we created a line of text in cell A1 that spilled over into cell B1. If you want the text to be contained in its cell, you need to use the wrap text function.

Wrap Text

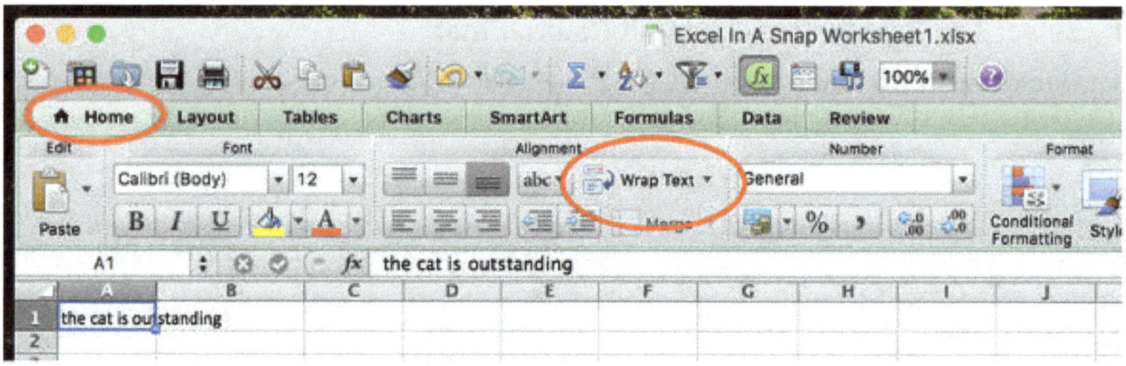

For Mac.   For Windows

1. Select cell A1.
2. On the Toolbar, look for <u>Wrap Text.</u>

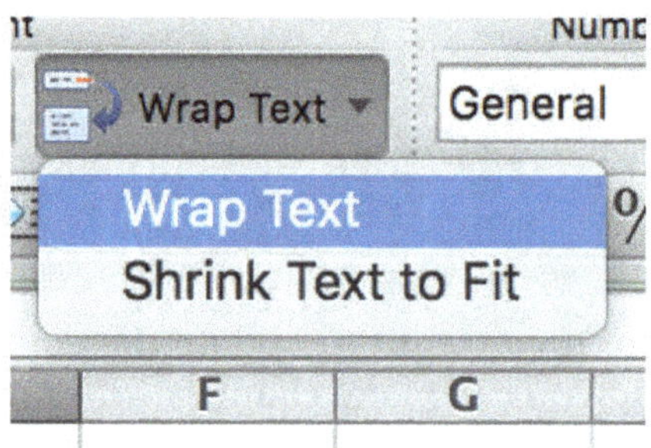

With the <u>Home</u> tab selected, look toward the middle of the ribbon. If you can't see the <u>Wrap Text</u> symbol, expand the window horizontally to bring it into view.

(Reminder: hover the pointer over the edge of the Excel window until it becomes a double horizontal arrow, and then click and drag to widen the window.)

Alternatively, you can scan the ribbon for the tiny logo of a white rectangle with a curved blue arrow, as shown above on the upper left.

The Windows version and most recent Mac versions display the green 'abc' logo on the upper far right.

3. Click the down arrow to the right and select <u>Wrap Text.</u>

Sometimes as you type in a specific cell, you may find that the row height automatically adjusts to the wrapped text, which means that cell has already been formatted to wrap text.

Remove Wrap Text Formatting

1. To remove wrap text formatting for a cell or range of cells, select the desired cells.

2. Click the <u>Wrap Text</u> symbol.

The Wrap Text symbol acts as a toggle such that you can turn the effect on and off with each click.

Adjust Row Height and Column Width With Click-and-Drag

If the cell has wrap text formatting, but you can see only one line:

1. Hover your pointer over the border between Row1 and Row2 until it turns into a double arrow as shown below.
2. Click and hold, then drag down until both lines come into view.

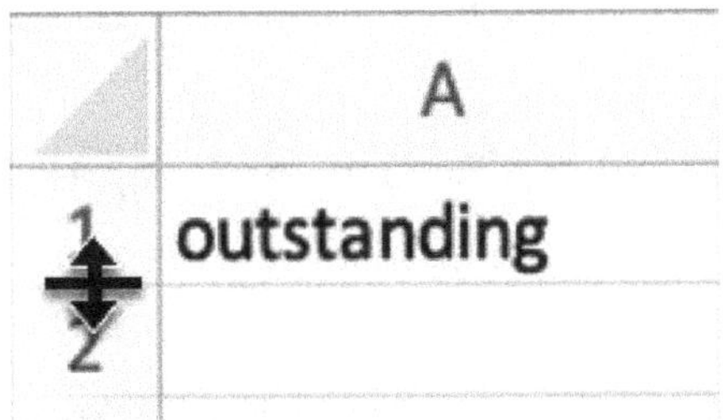

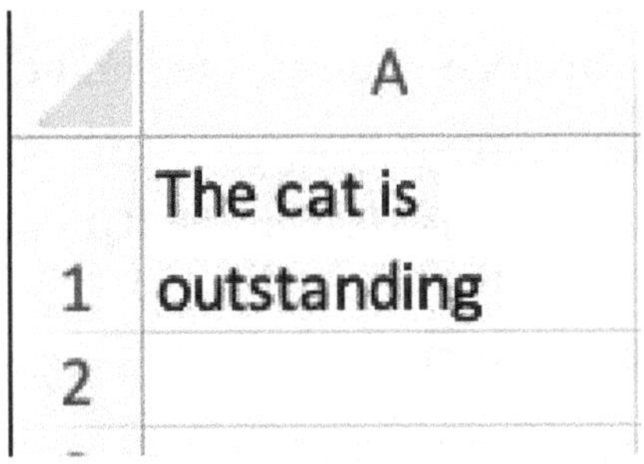

3. To adjust column width, hover your pointer on the border between Column A and B until it turns to a double arrow. Click-and-drag.

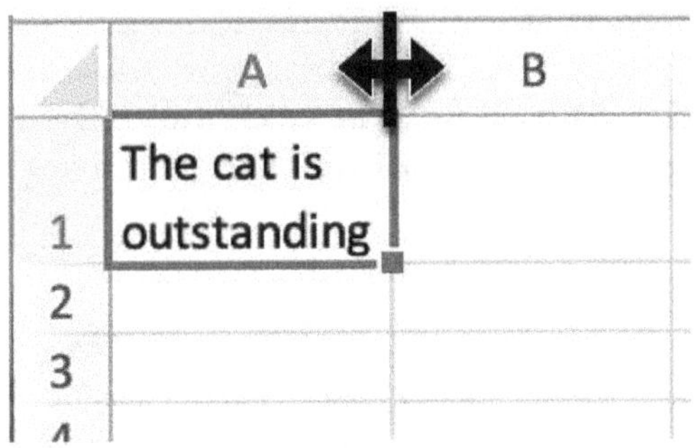

Adding Multiple Lines of Text Inside a Cell Using Line Breaks

For this exercise, you will be adding text to a cell to create a list with discrete line breaks.

1. Move your pointer to B1 and click.
2. Type "Shopping List:"
3. Enter a line break.
    - On a Mac, press-and-hold the <u>Option</u> key and <u>Control</u> key together, then hit <u>Return.</u>

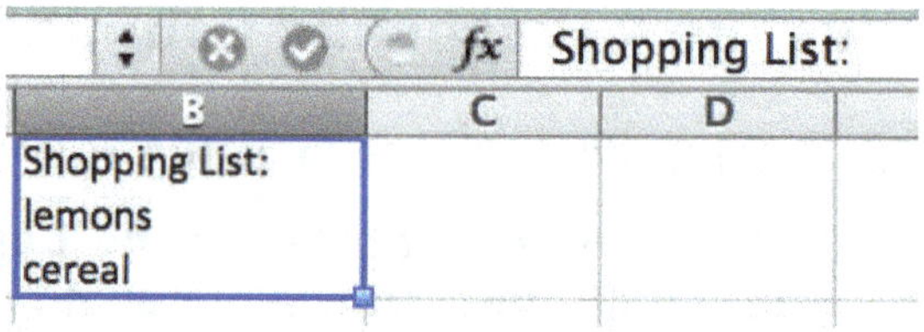

4. For Windows press and hold the <u>Alt</u> key and tap <u>Enter</u>.

Once a line break is entered, the cursor will move to the next line.

5. Type "lemons".
6. Enter another line break (Option + Control tap Return for Mac, Alt Enter for Windows).
7. Type "cereal".

You can also go to the Formula Bar, put your pointer at the end of "Shopping List:" and try it from there.

Expanding the Formula Bar

If the Formula Bar is not showing all of your text, move the pointer to the lower edge of the Formula Bar and hover until the pointer turns to a vertical double arrow with a middle bar. Click and drag down.

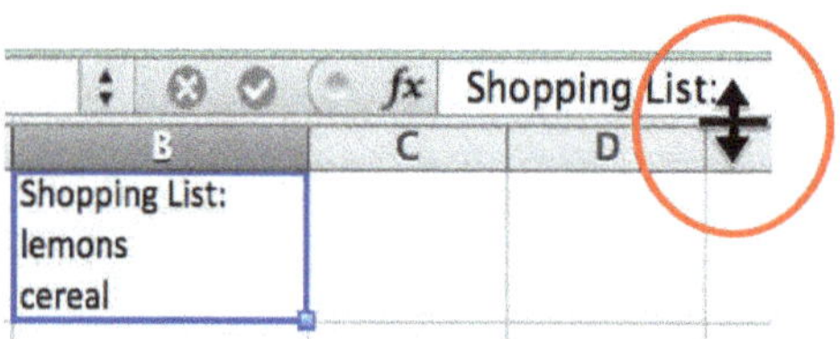

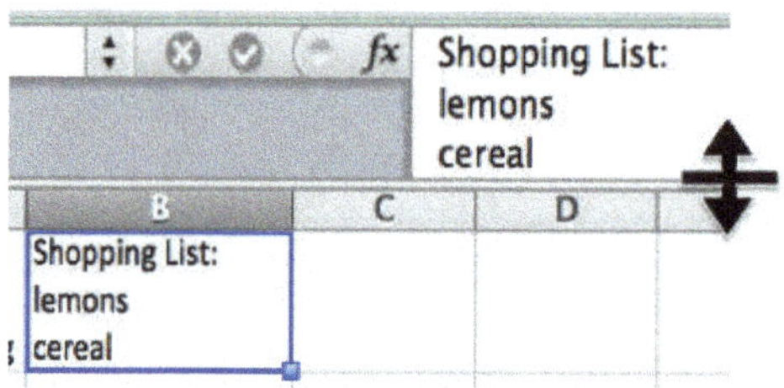

You can also widen columns using the same technique.

Undo and Redo

Excel makes it easy to undo your most recent edit. Look for the curved undo and redo arrows on the top toolbar of the Excel window (called the Quick Access menu).

Windows

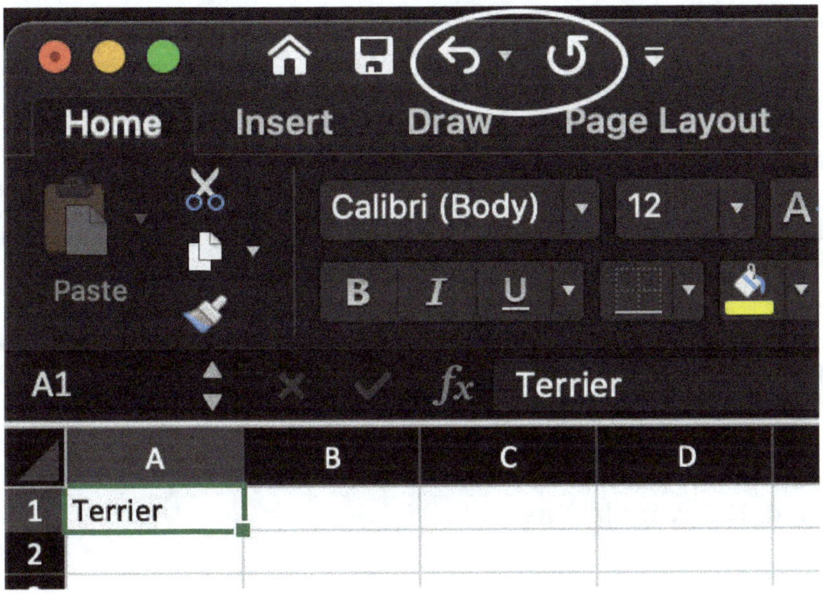

Mac

Tip: The Undo and Redo symbols on the most recent version of Excel for the Mac have arrows far more similar to those on the Windows version of Excel.

1. Click into cell A1.
2. Type the word Terrier.
3. Tap Return on Mac or Enter on Windows.
4. Click into cell A1 again. Type 'arf'
5. Hit Return on Mac or Enter on Windows.
6. Click the Undo button (left arrow).

Notice 'Terrier' replaces 'arf'.

7. Click the Redo button (right arrow).

Notice the word 'arf' appears again.

You can also execute the Undo and Redo commands from your Keyboard.

1. Hit □-Z for Undo (Control-Z for PCs.)
2. Hit □-Y for Redo. (Control-Y for PCs.)

The Undo/Redo Taskbar button and the Undo/Redo keystrokes are the same for most Microsoft software programs.

Undo History

You can display your Undo history by clicking on the small down arrow next to the Undo symbol to reveal the drop-down list.

To undo to a specific edit, select from the list. It is best to experiment with this tool on a practice worksheet. Never experiment on a worksheet that's part of a real project or program.

Cell Formatting Using the Menu

With the Home tab selected (top left of the Excel window), in the Font section, look for the formatting symbols for Bold, Italic, Underline, Color-fill, and Font Color.

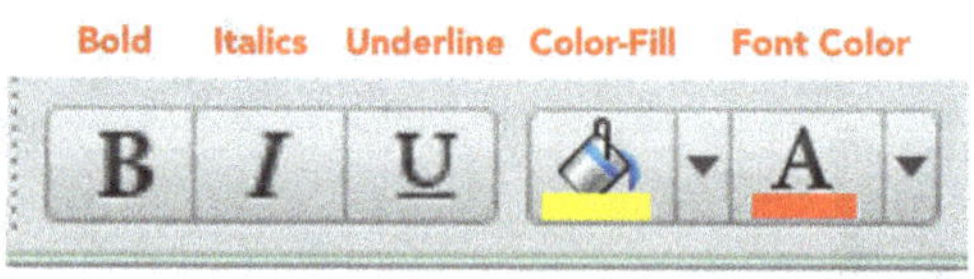

Similar tools are also found in other *Microsoft Office* applications.

1. **Click on the Bold symbol (letter B).**
2. **Click into cell C1 and type the word 'one'.**

Notice the word "one" is now bold

3. **Hit Return on Mac or Enter on Windows to move to the next cell down.**
4. **Type 'two', 'three' and 'four' into cells C2, C3, and C4, as shown.**
5. **Click back into cell C2 to select it and click on the Italic symbol (letter I).**

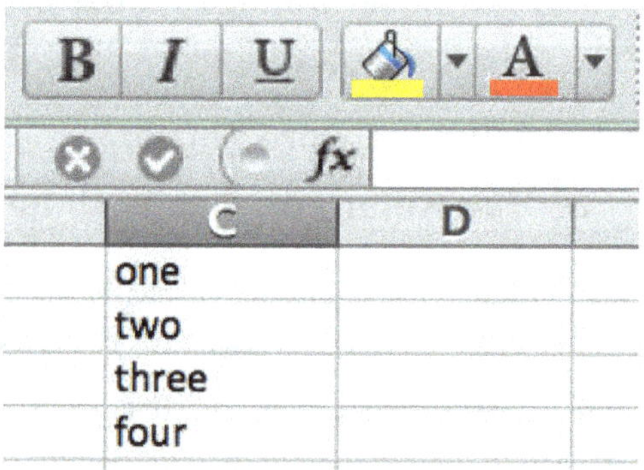

Tip: It is best to delete entire rows and columns rather than deleting a few cells and shifting cells up or down, right or left. If you do that in a large spreadsheet, you could misalign the remaining data and thereby damage the entire data set. Such a mistake could be hard to fix if not caught immediately.

Notice the text is now italicized.

6. Click on cell C3 and click the Underline symbol (letter U).

The text in this cell is now underlined.

7. Click on cell C4 and click the Font Color symbol (letter A).
8. Select the color red from the color menu on the bottom.

Notice the text is now red.

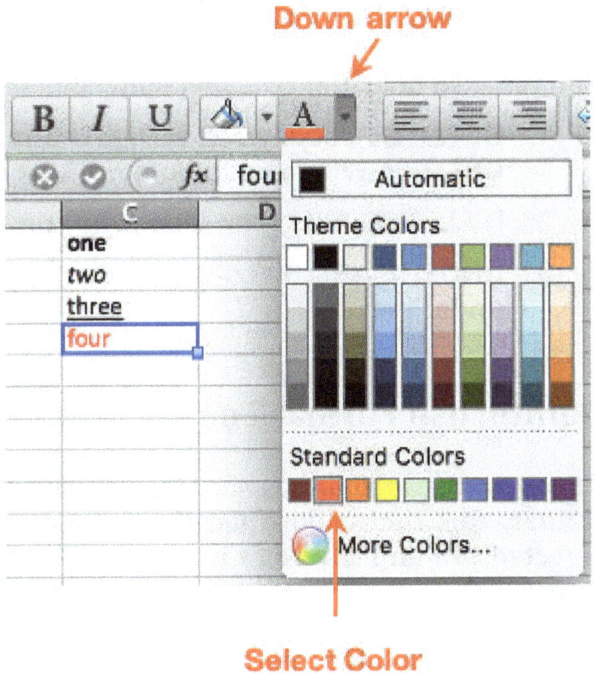

Now we're going to fill a cell with a color.

1. Select cell C3, the word *three.*
2. Click the down arrow on the Color-Fill symbol (paint bucket).

See image on the right.

3. Select the color yellow from the color menu at the bottom.

Notice cell C3 is now filled with yellow.

Cell Formatting Using the Keyboard

You can also bold, italicize, and underline text using your keyboard.

1. **BOLD: Select any cell with text and press <u>□-B</u> on Mac, or <u>Ctrl-B</u> on Windows to bold the text in that cell.**
2. **ITALICIZE: Hit <u>□-I</u> on Mac, <u>Ctrl-I</u> on Windows to italicize.**
3. **UNDERLINE: Hit <u>□-U</u> on Mac, <u>Ctrl-U</u> on Windows to underline.**

Paintbrush Format Tool

The Paintbrush tool has nothing to do with color. Rather, this tool copies just the formatting of the selected cell and transfers it to the cell or cells you select next.

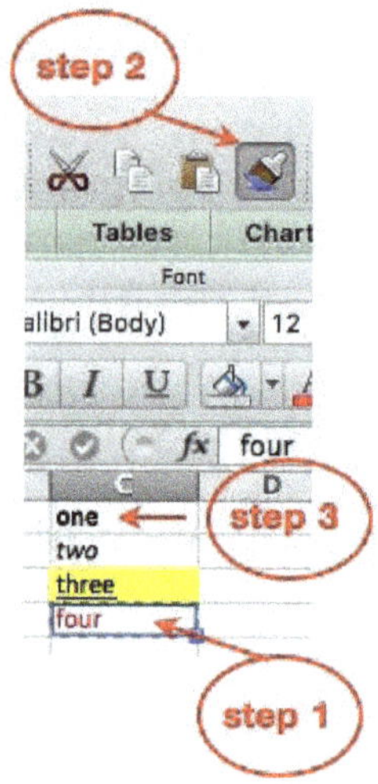

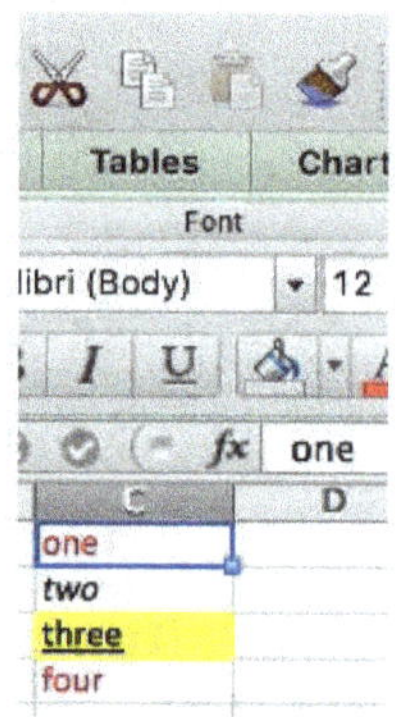

With the <u>Home</u> tab selected, you should find the <u>Paintbrush</u> symbol on the ribbon in the upper left region.

1. **Click on <u>cell C4</u> (the word f*our*) to select it.**
2. **Click on the <u>Paintbrush</u> symbol.**

Notice the cell C4 now has "marching ants" (moving dashes) around it. Also, the pointer changes to a plus-sign and a paintbrush symbol.

3. **Click on cell C1.**

Notice the word *one* in cell C1 is now in red font, like the word 'four' in C4.

This method works for all formatting commands. For example, if text in a cell is formatted as bold, underlined, and font color, the formatting paintbrush will apply all of the text formatting in the source cell to the target cells.

Copy, Cut, and Paste Cells Using Right-Click

Even if you are familiar with the copy-and-paste tool from other software, you should run through these exercises since the process may be different in Excel.

1. **Click on cell C1, (the word 'one').**
2. **Right-click (on your mouse click button to the right).**
3. **On the pop-up menu, select <u>Copy</u>.**

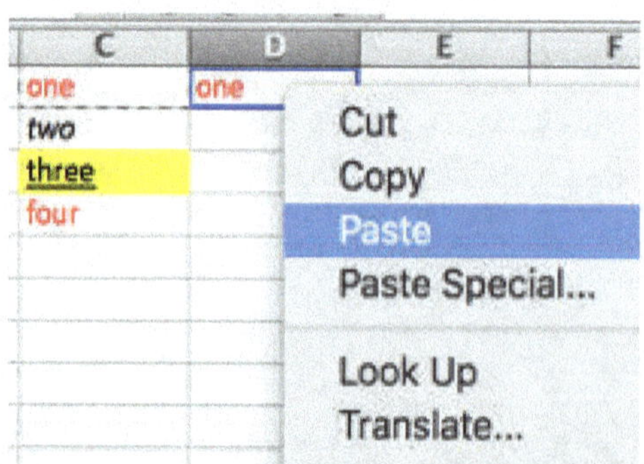

4. Click on cell D1 to select.
5. Right-click on cell D1 and select Paste.

Notice after pasting cells, the copied cells will still have marching ants.

To get rid of marching ants:

1. Hit the Escape key on the far-upper-left of your keyboard.
2. Look for the letters “esc”.

Note: If you are using a Mac and have not set your mouse to enable right-clicks, instead of right-clicking, hold down the Control key, and then click.

Copy and Paste Cells using Keyboard

To copy and paste a single cell:

1. Click on cell C2 (the word *two*) to select it.
2. On your Keyboard, hit □-C on Mac, Ctrl-C on Windows, (press and hold the □ Key and press letter ‘C’) to copy.
3. Click into cell D2.
4. Hit □-V to paste on Mac, Ctrl-V on Windows.

Cut and Paste Cells using Keyboard

To cut and paste cells:

1. Click on cell C2 (the word two) to select it.
2. On your Keyboard, hit □-X on Mac, Ctrl-X on Windows, (press and hold the □ Key and press letter ‘X’) to cut.
3. Click into an empty cell.
4. Use □-V to paste on Mac, or Ctrl-V on Windows, whether you are copying or cutting.

Copy and Paste Multiple Cells

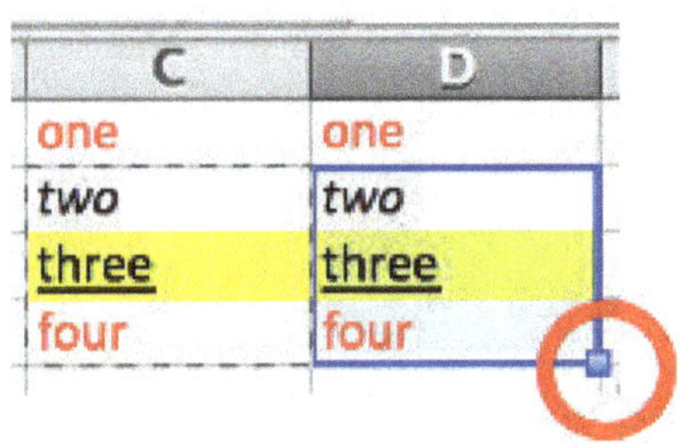

1. Click-and-hold on cell C2 and then drag down to select the next two cells below.
2. Look for the tiny square on the lower right corner of the cell pointer (blue rectangle).

3. **Hover the cursor over the square until it becomes a black plus sign. Click-and-hold, then drag to the right. Or you can drag down.**

This copies the contents of cells C2-C4, in order, to all other cells in the cell pointer (the blue rectangle created by the selection).

Notice the Copy-and-Paste command copies formatting along with the text. Go ahead and play around with this function to get comfortable with it.

Caution: When pasting multiple cells, ensure that the content does not overlap with adjacent cells to prevent unintended data loss. Keep in mind that pasted cells will automatically overwrite any existing content in the target area.

Copy, Cut, and Paste Using the App Menu Bar (For Mac only)

1. **Select the cell or cells to be copied.**
2. **Click Edit on the App Menu Bar.**
3. **Scroll down the drop-down menu and click Copy.**
4. **Select the cell that you wish to place the copied material.**

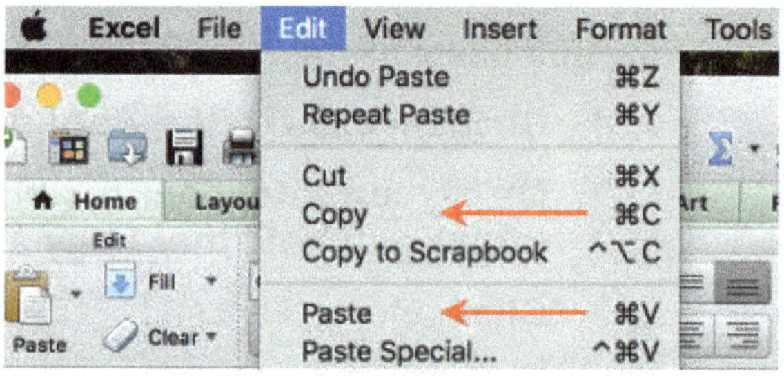

5. **Again, click on Edit on the App Menu Bar, but this time click Paste.**

Text and Cell Alignment

Excel text usually defaults to align left within the cells. You can use the alignment tools to align right or center your text. You'll find them in the Alignment section of the Excel "Home" menu tab to the right of the text formatting tools. Select one of the text cells and play around with the alignment tools.

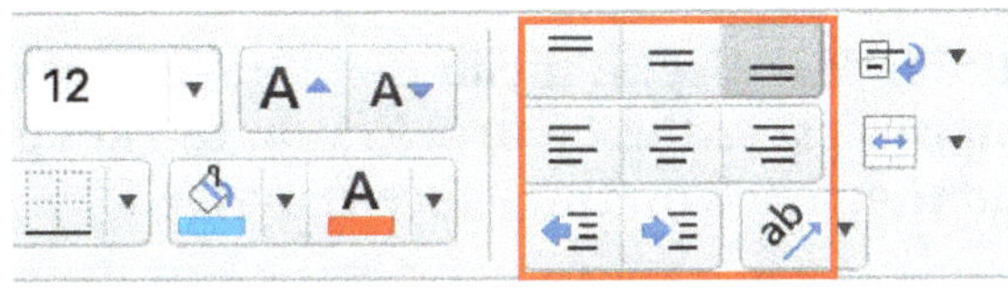

Angled and Vertical Text

If you are going to experiment with the text angle tool (look for the symbol with the letters 'ab' at an angle as shown above) you need to know how to undo your work so you don't get stuck with sandbox formatting.

Use the angled or vertical text tool as seldom as possible. It's best to avoid using it altogether on a living document that is frequently updated. If you merge multiple cells with vertical or angled text, the result will be unnecessarily tall rows that will be confusing. Also, it can interfere with inserting or deleting rows, columns, and other functionality. As with any good design, it's best to stick with the old KISS adage—*Keep It Super Simple*.

Nonetheless, familiarizing yourself with the text angle tool is a good idea. Angled or vertical text can be handy on flyers, brochures, and other business collateral.

1. Select a word and click on the Text Angle tool and select Vertical Text.

Feel free to go into sandbox mode and experiment with this tool. You may have to expand a row to see vertical text.

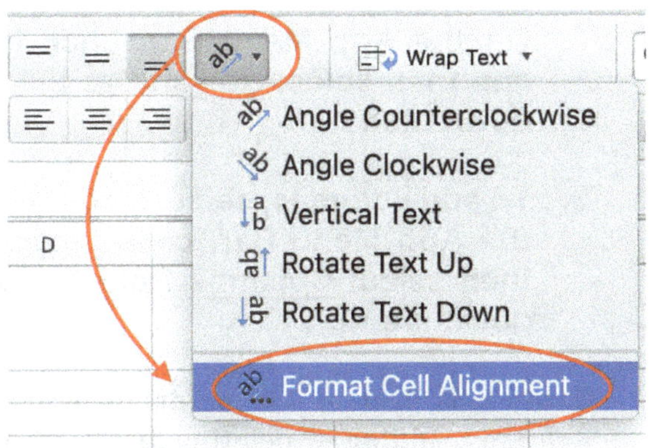

2. To return vertical text to horizontal, just click on Vertical Text again to unselect it.
3. To restore the angled text to horizontal: Click the Text Angle tool and Format Cell Alignment.
4. In the drop-down (see the images on the right), you can either move the text needle to the horizontal position. Or you can simply clear the box next to Degrees: and enter 0 (zero).
5. Click OK.

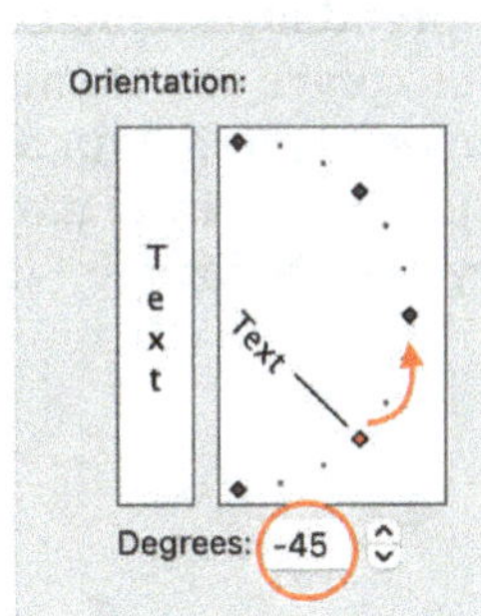

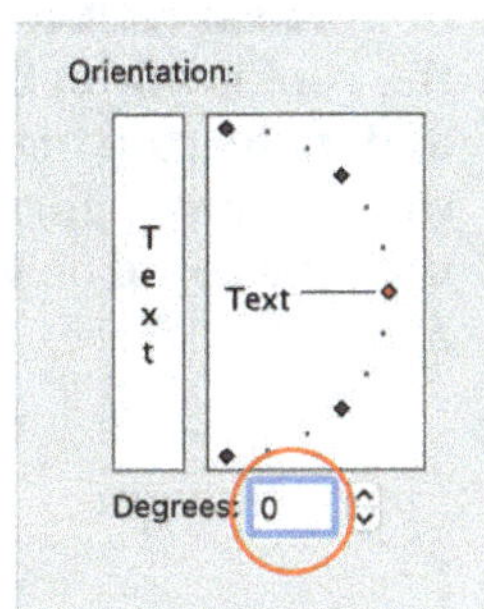

This will restore the text to its original horizontal alignment.

Add and Delete Rows and Columns By Right-Click

TIP for Mac Users: If you don't have access to right-click on your mouse or touchpad, you can press the Control key on the keypad and then click on the selected material.

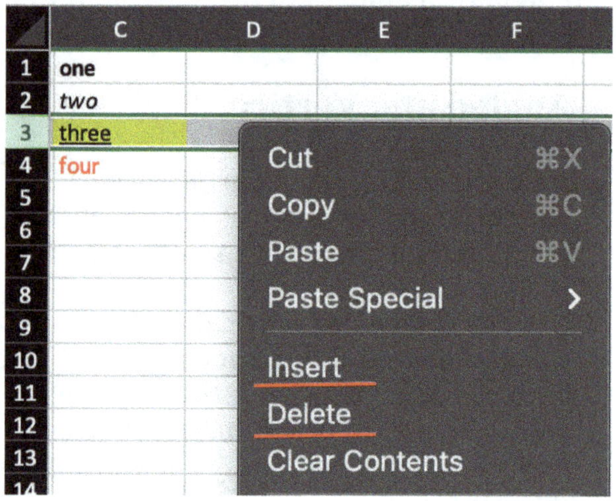

1. **Select row 3. (Hover your pointer over the numeral 3 until it becomes a black arrow. Click to select.**
2. **Right-click and from the pop-up menu, select <u>Insert</u>.**
3. **To delete the new row, select it, Right-click, and choose <u>Delete</u>.**
4. **To add and delete columns, select Column B then follow the directions above.**

Add and Delete Rows From the App Menu Bar (Macs only)

1. **Select a row by clicking on the row number.**
2. **On the App Menu Bar, click <u>Insert</u> and then select <u>Rows</u> from the drop down menu.**
3. **To add columns, select a column. On the App Menu Bar, click <u>Insert</u> and then select <u>Columns</u> from the drop-down menu.**

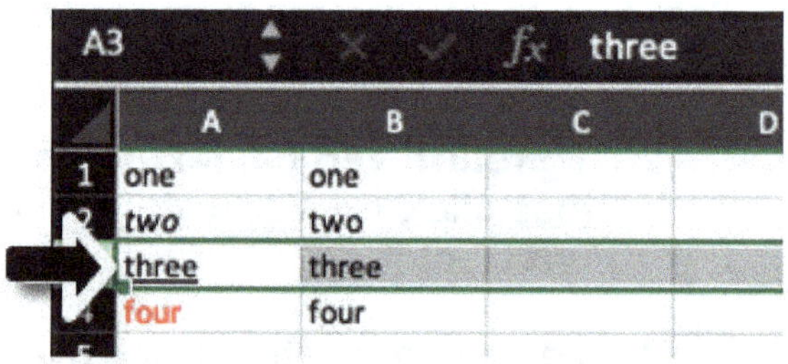

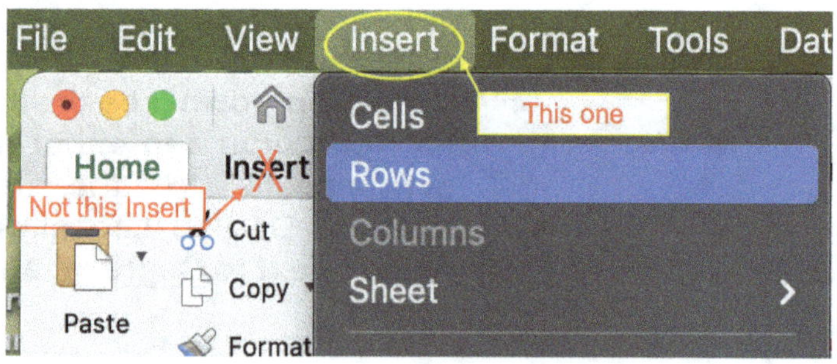

Tip: It is best to add or delete entire rows or columns. Adding or deleting just a few horizontal or vertical cells in a spreadsheet, and then shifting the remaining cells into place can throw off a table of data by causing the remaining data to align with the wrong corresponding information. This mistake could be very hard to fix if not caught right away.

4. **To delete, select the rowà<u>Edit</u>à<u>Delete</u>.**

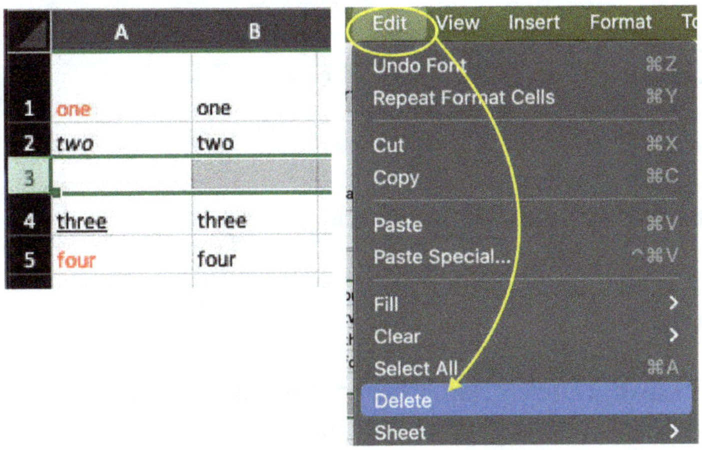

Clear Formatting

Tip: The cell's formatting remains even if the contents are erased or replaced. You can either clear specific formatting, or you can clear all formatting at once.

Clear All Formatting

You can quickly clear all formatting from the App Menu Bar (at the very top of the screen on a Mac).

1. **EditàClearàFormats**

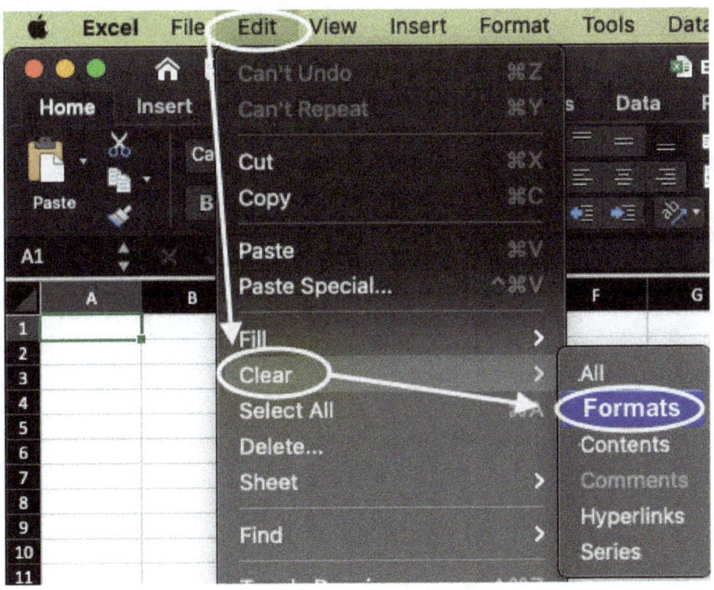

Clear Font Color

1. Click on cell D1.

2. On the Font Color symbol (letter A), click the down-arrow.

3. Choose Automatic.

This will change the font to the default color black.

Clear Text Bold and Italics

1. To clear the bold and italic styles, select the cell with Bold or Italic text and click the Bold symbol, or the Italic symbol.

2. On your Keyboard, hit □-B on Mac, or Ctrl-B for Windows to clear Bold formatting, or □-I for Italic on Mac or Ctrl-I on windows.

Both function as a toggle, or on-and-off switch.

Clear Formatting Using Paintbrush Tool:

We will replace the formatting with that found in cell D1, plain black text.

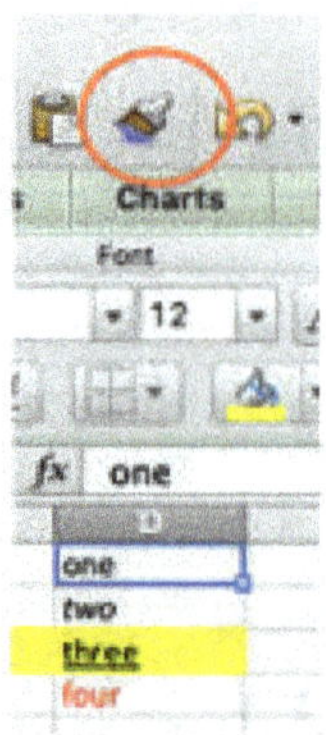

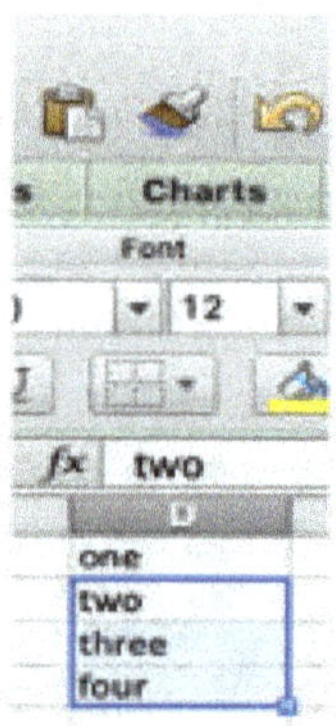

1. Click on the word "one" in cell D1.

2. Click on the Paintbrush tool.

3. Place your pointer over the word "two" in cell D2.

4. Click-and-drag to select the words *two, three, and four.*

   You can also use the paintbrush tool to copy the formatting of a blank cell that still has the default formatting, and then apply it to the target cells.

Clear Cell Contents and Formatting—Short Cut

If you don't have a large amount of content in your worksheet, and you want to clear it, there is a quick and easy way to do this with the *Copy-and-Paste* function.

1. **Place your pointer in cell E5 or someplace where the cells are clear.**

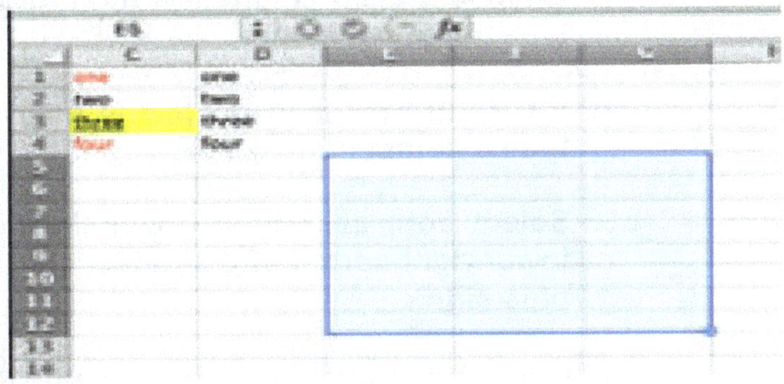

2. **Click and drag three cells to the right and down to row 12.**
3. **Tap □-C on Mac or Ctrl-C on Windows to copy.**
4. **Place your pointer in cell C1, on the word 'one' in red font.**

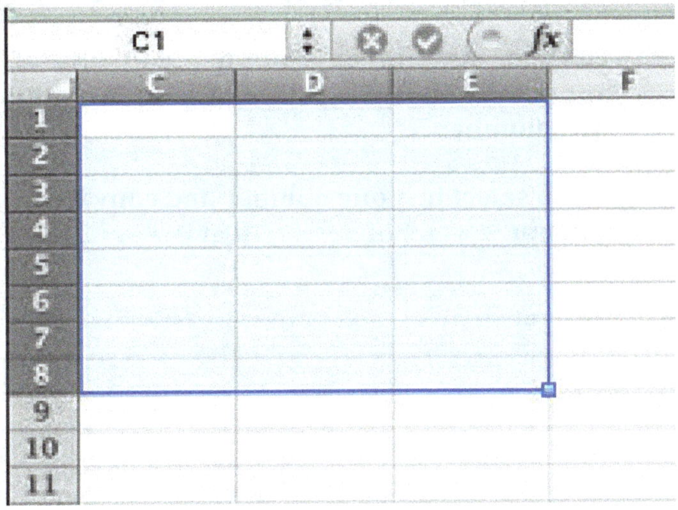

5. **On your keyboard, tap □-V on Mac, or Ctrl-V on Windows to paste.**

The blank cells overwrite the pre-existing text, and the formatting reverts to the default format. This is a handy shortcut to get rid of both the text and the formatting.

6. **Click □-Z on Mac, or Ctrl-Z if you want to undo the change.**

Create a Column of Consecutive Numbers

It is easy to create a column of consecutive numbers in Excel.

1. **Choose a clear column. In the first row or top cell, type a number 1.**

2. **Hit Return/Enter to go to the next cell below and type a number 2.**

3. **Select both cells then hover the pointer over the lower right corner of the selection until it turns to a plus sign.**

4. **Click and drag the selection down to create the column of consecutive numbers.**

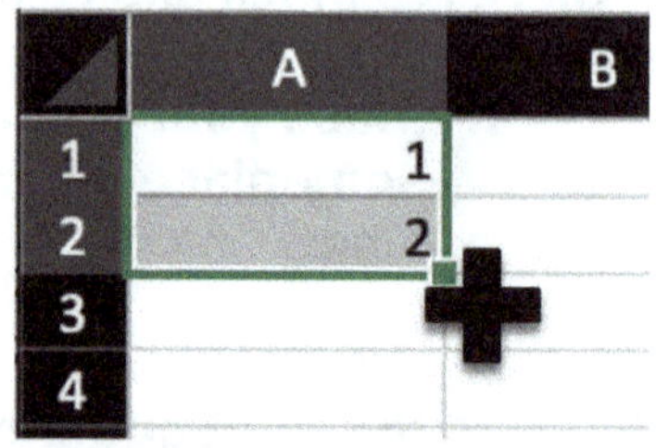

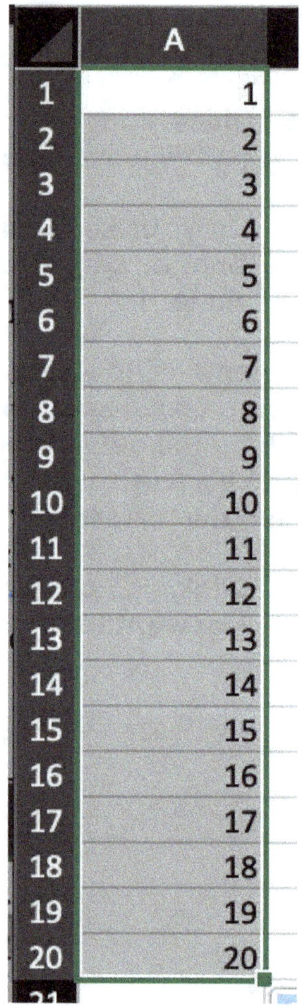

You can start at any number you like. If you start with number 5 and 6, you will get a column of numbers that starts with number 5.

If you select just one number and copy it down, you will get a column of just that number.

PROJECT 1: Stakeholder List

Stakeholder lists are used to keep track of key personnel on a large project and are designed for sorting and filtering information. The list for this exercise will be far smaller than a real stakeholder list, but it will serve as a sampler for commonly used Excel formatting and sorting functions.

If you want to access the *Excel In A Snap Project Workbook* file, please go to our website at: INaSnapGuides.com, and download the file Excel In A Snap Project Worksheets. At the bottom of the workbook, select the worksheet labeled, 1. Stakeholder List.

The Excel In a Snap Project Workbooks file contains sheets for all 8 projects.

If you'd prefer to make the stakeholder list from scratch, use the following instructions.

1. **Go to the bottom of the Excel window to the Sheet labels and click the plus sign to create a new sheet.**
2. **Double-click on the tab label and type the words "Stakeholder List".**

3. **Fill out the new worksheet as shown below.**

	A	B	C	D	E	F	G
1	Stakeholder List						
2	Name	Department	Supervisor	City	Team A	Team B	Notes
3	Daiyu, Tony	Sales	Jennifer Hill	Austin		x	
4	Gomez, Miguel	Business	Michael Delgado	Austin	x		
5	Aishwarya, Amrita	Engineering	Alex Shim	Austin		x	
6	Edelson, Lemar			St. Louis	x		
7	Ingersol, Larry			St. Louis		x	
8	Han, Marisa			St. Louis	x		
9	Brown, Tonya			Minneapolis		x	
10	Ford, Frank			Minneapolis	x		
11	Carter, Mel			Minneapolis		x	

Adjust Row Height and Column Width With Double-Click

In earlier exercises, we sized columns and rows by hovering the pointer over the line between either the column headers or the row numbers, and then applying the click-and-drag maneuver.

This time, we're going to explore different methods of sizing rows and columns.

1. **Hover your pointer in the column header bar on the boundary between columns A and B until the pointer becomes a double arrow.**
2. **Click and drag the boundary right and left to manually change the column's width.**
3. **Keeping the pointer on the column boundary, let go of the mouse button, and then double-click.**

The column border should automatically move to display the longest line of text in the column

If you have text with more than one line in a cell, but only one line showing, you can use the same double-click method on the boundary between row labels to increase the row's height.

1. **To try this out, place the word 'List' on a second line. (Reminder: Use Option+Control and Return on Mac, or Alt-Return on Windows to add a line break inside the cell.)**
2. **Hover the pointer in the row number bar on the boundary between rows 1 and 2 until it turns to the double-arrow. Double-click.**

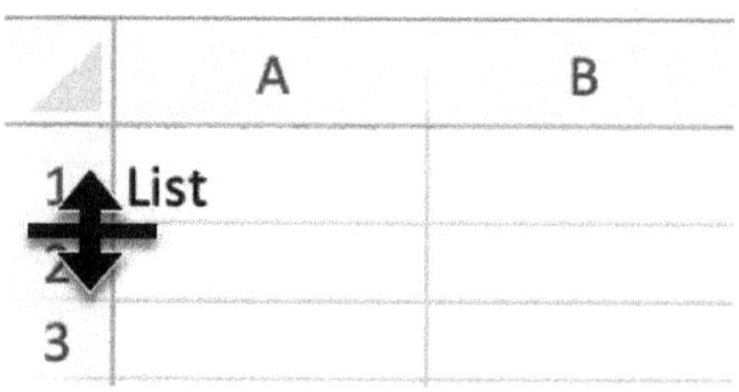

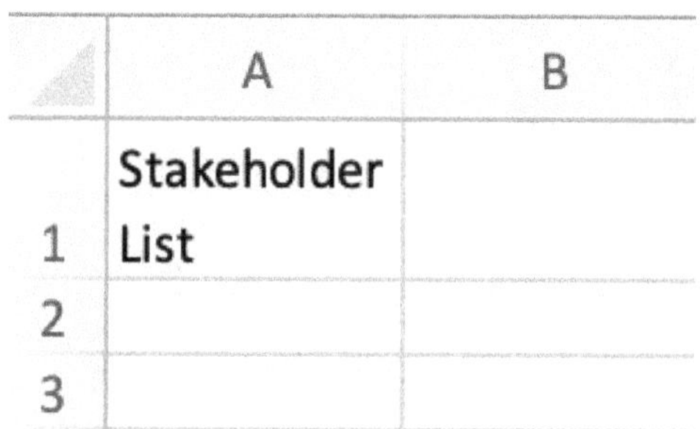

Make Columns and Rows a Uniform Size With Right-Click

Sometimes you need many columns on your worksheet to be of uniform width, and the rows to be a uniform height. You can achieve this using either right-click or from the App Menu Bar.

1. Hover your cursor over the lower edge of the column header bar for column A until it changes to a down arrow.

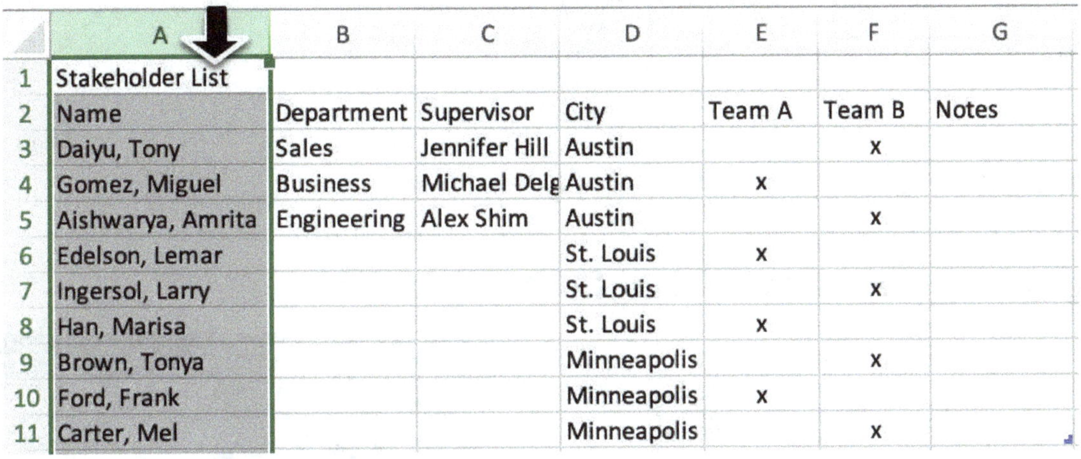

	A	B	C	D	E	F	G
1	Stakeholder List						
2	Name	Department	Supervisor	City	Team A	Team B	Notes
3	Daiyu, Tony	Sales	Jennifer Hill	Austin		x	
4	Gomez, Miguel	Business	Michael Delg	Austin	x		
5	Aishwarya, Amrita	Engineering	Alex Shim	Austin		x	
6	Edelson, Lemar			St. Louis	x		
7	Ingersol, Larry			St. Louis		x	
8	Han, Marisa			St. Louis	x		
9	Brown, Tonya			Minneapolis		x	
10	Ford, Frank			Minneapolis	x		
11	Carter, Mel			Minneapolis		x	

2. Click and drag over Columns A, B, C, D, E, F and G to select them.

3. Right-click on the selected cells and from the pop-up menu choose Column Width.

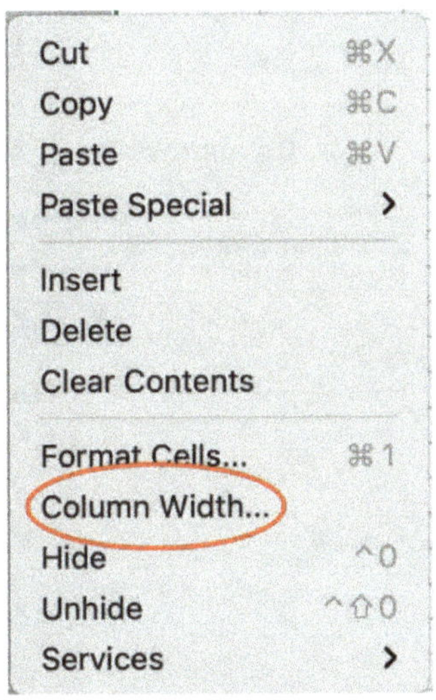

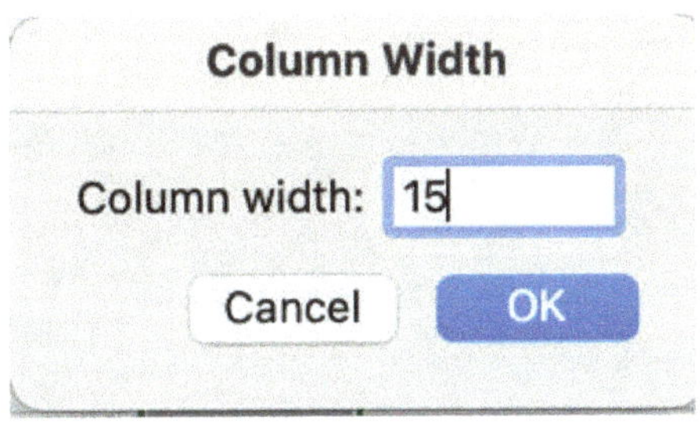

4. In the Column Width box, enter 15.

Tip: If you get a strange result with that figure, then hit □-Zto undo, and try again with 1.25".

	A	B	C	D	E	F	G
1	Stakeholder List						
2	Name	Department	Supervisor	City	Team A	Team B	Notes
3	Daiyu, Tony	Sales	Jennifer Hill	Austin		x	
4	Gomez, Miguel	Business	Michael Delgado	Austin	x		
5	Aishwarya, Amrita	Engineering	Alex Shim	Austin		x	
6	Edelson, Lemar			St. Louis	x		
7	Ingersol, Larry			St. Louis		x	
8	Han, Marisa			St. Louis	x		
9	Brown, Tonya			Minneapolis		x	
10	Ford, Frank			Minneapolis	x		
11	Carter, Mel			Minneapolis		x	

When you're done, your table should look like the one above.

Sizing Columns and Rows From the Menu Bar on Mac

1. **For Mac users, go to the App Menu (very top of your computer screen) click <u>Format</u> à <u>Column</u> à <u>Width.</u>**

   Windows users will find the format tab at the top of the application's window.

2. **In the Column Width pop-up enter 15 (or 1.24" for earlier Excel version).**

3. **Click <u>OK</u> or hit <u>Return/Enter</u>.**

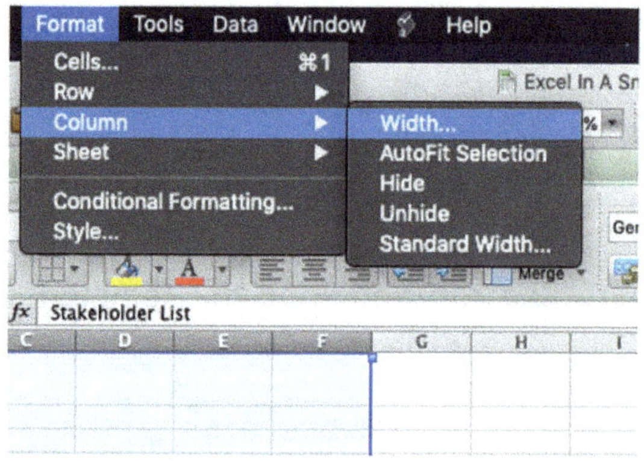

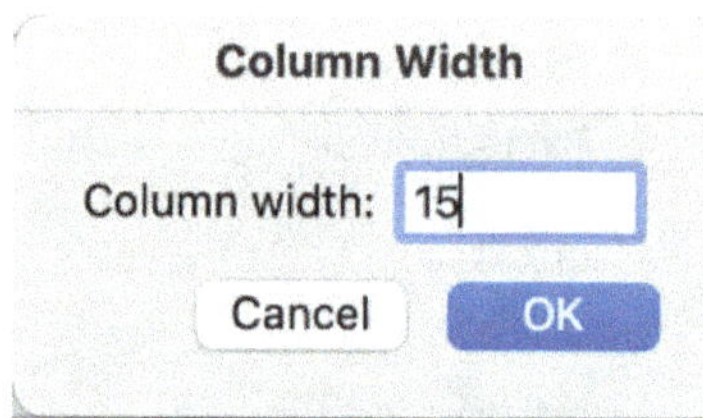

Copy and Paste Multiple Cells Using Click-and-Drag

Now let's fill in our worksheet.

1. In column B, under Department, click and hold on "Sales" in B3, then drag the pointer down two more cells to select B4 and B5, and release.
2. Look for the tiny square at the lower right of the Cell Pointer.
3. Hover your pointer over the tiny square until it becomes a plus-sign.
4. Click-and-hold to drag it down to cell B11 and let go.

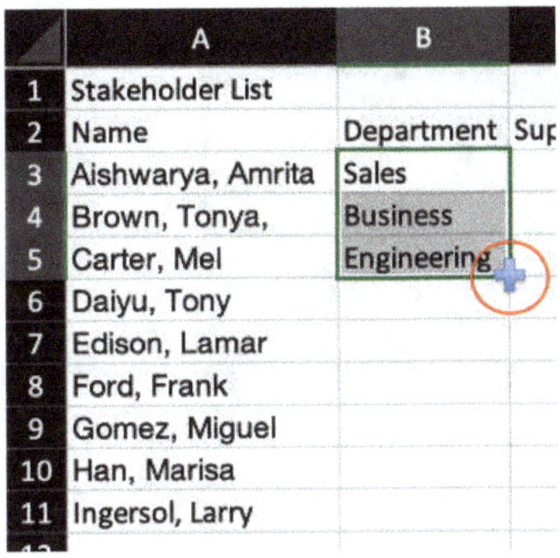

	A	B
1	Stakeholder List	
2	Name	Department
3	Aishwarya, Amrita	Sales
4	Brown, Tonya,	Business
5	Carter, Mel	Engineering
6	Daiyu, Tony	
7	Edison, Lamar	
8	Ford, Frank	
9	Gomez, Miguel	
10	Han, Marisa	
11	Ingersol, Larry	

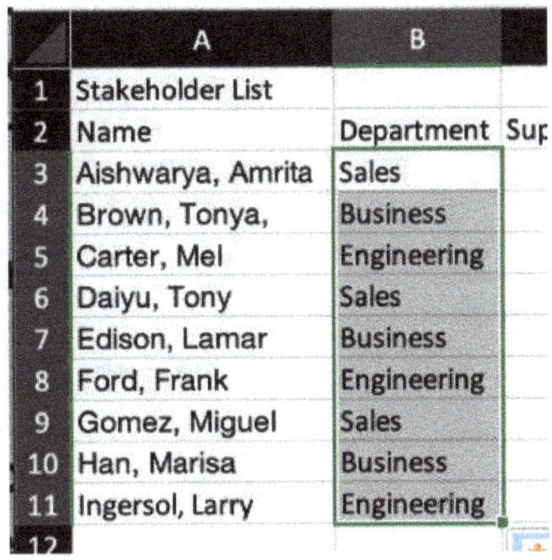

	A	B
1	Stakeholder List	
2	Name	Department
3	Aishwarya, Amrita	Sales
4	Brown, Tonya,	Business
5	Carter, Mel	Engineering
6	Daiyu, Tony	Sales
7	Edison, Lamar	Business
8	Ford, Frank	Engineering
9	Gomez, Miguel	Sales
10	Han, Marisa	Business
11	Ingersol, Larry	Engineering

Notice all three words copied in sequence. In a real scenario it is unlikely the departments would fall in line so neatly, this is just an exercise to demonstrate how to copy-and-paste multiple cells.

5. Repeat this exercise in column C to copy the three supervisors to the bottom of the table.

When you are done, your table should look like the one below.

	A	B	C	D	E	F	G
1	Stakeholder List						
2	Name	Department	Supervisor	City	Team A	Team B	Notes
3	Daiyu, Tony	Sales	Jennifer Hill	Austin		x	
4	Gomez, Miguel	Business	Michael Delgado	Austin	x		
5	Aishwarya, Amrita	Engineering	Alex Shim	Austin		x	
6	Edelson, Lemar	Sales	Jennifer Hill	St. Louis	x		
7	Ingersol, Larry	Business	Michael Delgado	St. Louis		x	
8	Han, Marisa	Engineering	Alex Shim	St. Louis	x		
9	Brown, Tonya	Sales	Jennifer Hill	Minneapolis		x	
10	Ford, Frank	Business	Michael Delgado	Minneapolis	x		
11	Carter, Mel	Engineering	Alex Shim	Minneapolis		x	

Formatting Table Headers

Let's give this table a decent header.

1. **Horizontally select cells A1-G1.**
2. **Make sure the ribbon's <u>Home</u> tab is selected, and in the ribbon's Alignment section, locate the Merge & Center symbol (a small grid with a blue double arrow; see screenshot below on left).**
3. **Click the down arrow next to the Merge & Center Symbol and select "Merge & Center." This will cause the selected cells to merge, and center-align "Stakeholder List."**

Merge & Center Icon

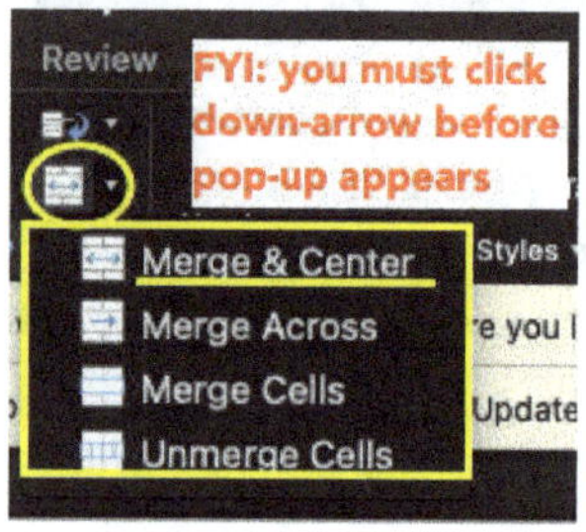

With the newly merged cell (and the words "Stakeholder List") still selected,

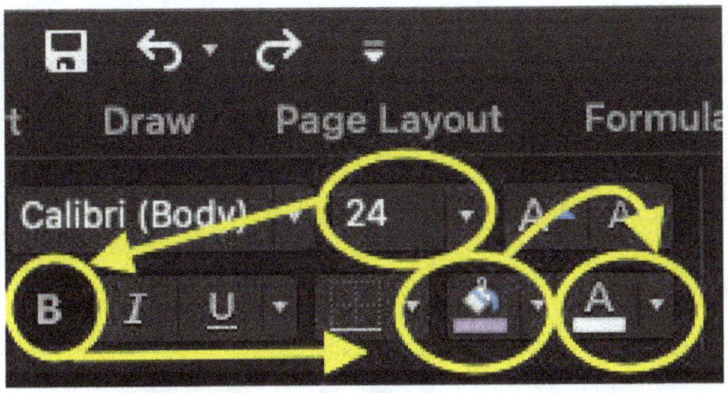

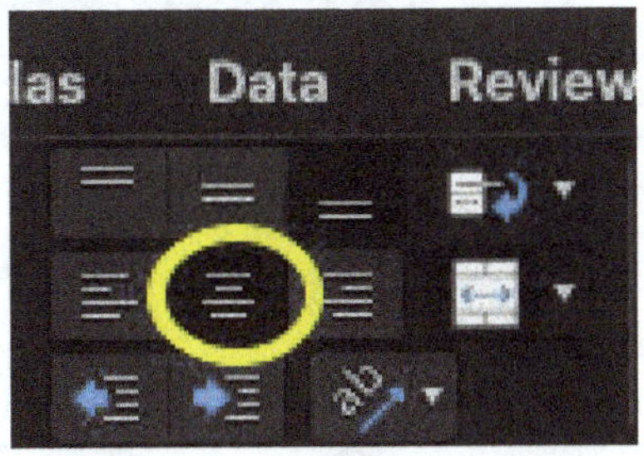

1. **To change the font size of the text, find the Font section of the ribbon (see screenshot above) and click on the down arrow at the right edge of the Font Size box. From the drop-down menu, select 24.**
2. **Bold the text by clicking the 'B' symbol in the Font section of the ribbon.**
3. **To fill the cell with a specific color, find the Paint Bucket symbol, click the down arrow, and select a dark color—a dull shade of gray, blue, or green will serve the purposes of this lesson.**
4. **To change the color of the font, click the down arrow next to the Font Color symbol (the letter A above a color bar, see above) and select the color white.**
5. **Center the text by selecting the Center Align symbol located in the Alignment section of the ribbon (see screenshot above on the right).**
6. **Select cells in the second row: A2-G2.**
7. **Bold the text by clicking on "B" in the ribbon.**
8. **Click on the Paint Bucket tool and select a pale shade of the same fill color you used on the top header.**

Your stakeholder list should look something like the image below. This is a simplified version of a Stakeholder List, but you will learn the basic tools you'll need to add and sort information on a far larger and more complex stakeholder document.

Stakeholder List						
Name	**Department**	**Supervisor**	**City**	**Team A**	**Team B**	**Notes**
Daiyu, Tony	Sales	Jennifer Hill	Austin		x	
Gomez, Miguel	Business	Michael Delgado	Austin	x		
Aishwarya, Amrita	Engineering	Alex Shim	Austin		x	
Edelson, Lemar	Sales	Jennifer Hill	St. Louis	x		
Ingersol, Larry	Business	Michael Delgado	St. Louis		x	
Han, Marisa	Engineering	Alex Shim	St. Louis	x		
Brown, Tonya	Sales	Jennifer Hill	Minneapolis		x	
Ford, Frank	Business	Michael Delgado	Minneapolis	x		
Carter, Mel	Engineering	Alex Shim	Minneapolis		x	

Tip: In a professional setting it's best to use muted colors. Bright colors tend to be distracting.

Add A Border To A Table On A Mac

1. **Select the entire table, A1 through H11 by clicking on A1 and dragging to H11.**

2. **On the Font section of the Home ribbon, click the down-arrow on the <u>Border</u> symbol (the divided square, circled in screenshot).**

3. **In the drop-down menu, select <u>Thick Box Border</u>.**

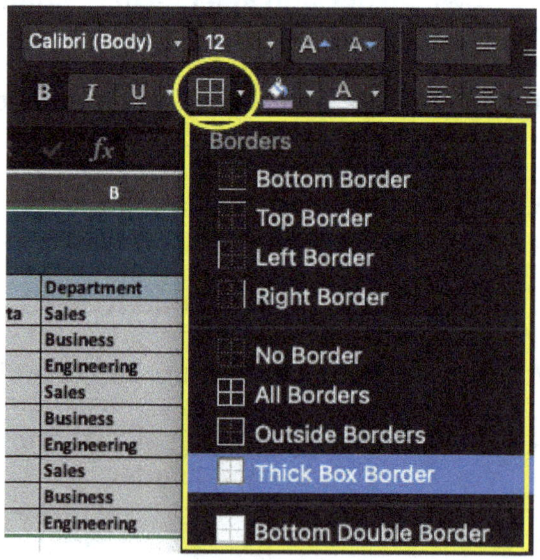

Add A Border To A Table On Windows

1. Select the entire table by clicking on A1 and dragging to H11.

2. With the Home tab selected, look for the Font section of the ribbon and click the small angled arrow in the lower-right corner of the font toolbox (see screenshot below on the right).

3. In the pop-up window (below) select the Border tab, then select the Outline symbol, then, under Style, select the line style. If you want to choose a color, click the down arrow on the Color field, select a color, then click OK when you're done.

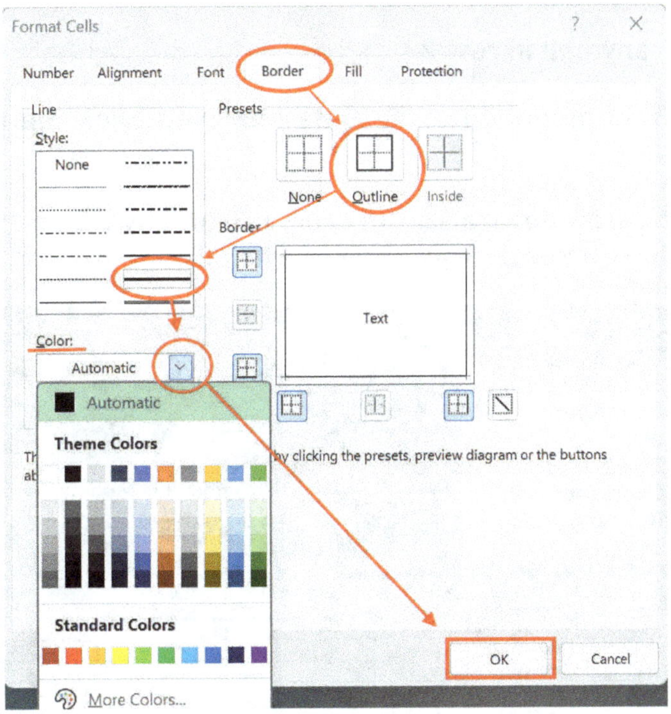

Sort and Filter Functions

Tip! Keep in mind that when you open Excel it always defaults to the **Home** *tab which is where you will find the most commonly used tools.*

Once you click another tab—such as **Data**—*you need to remember that you are on a completely different ribbon. So, if you cannot find basic functions, like the font tools etc., remember to click back on the* **Home** *tab.*

Sorting and filtering allows you to access specific information on a worksheet. You can use sorting to put lists in alphanumeric order, or to bring certain categories to the top of a list. Filtering allows you to screen out everything except the information you are seeking.

Add Sort/Filter Arrows To Category Row

1. **Click into any cell in row 2.**
2. **On the Excel menu, click the Data tab, then click the filter symbol (see below).**

This will put a drop-down arrow in every cell in Row 2. Now that every category has a drop-down arrow, let's play around with this.

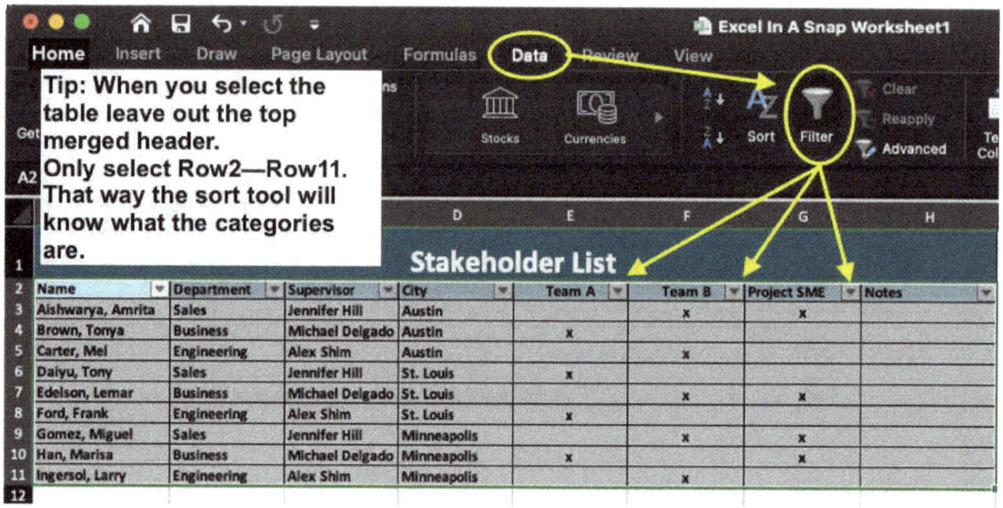

Sort Alphabetically

1. **Click on the drop-down arrow on the Name cell.**
2. **In the drop-down window click the Ascending option.**

This automatically puts the entries in the Name column in alphabetical order.

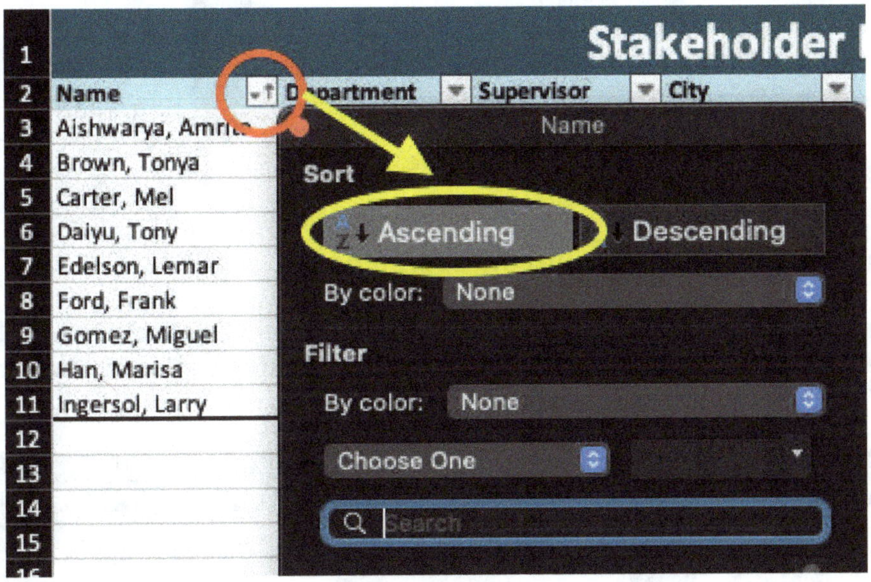

In the screenshot above, notice that in cell A2, next to the word "Name", the triangular down-arrow has an upward-pointing arrow beside it. This tells us that the Name column is sorted in ascending order. The entries in the corresponding columns will align with the Name column. For most stakeholder lists, an alphabetized Name column as a default mode is preferred.

Filter for a Specific Name or Category

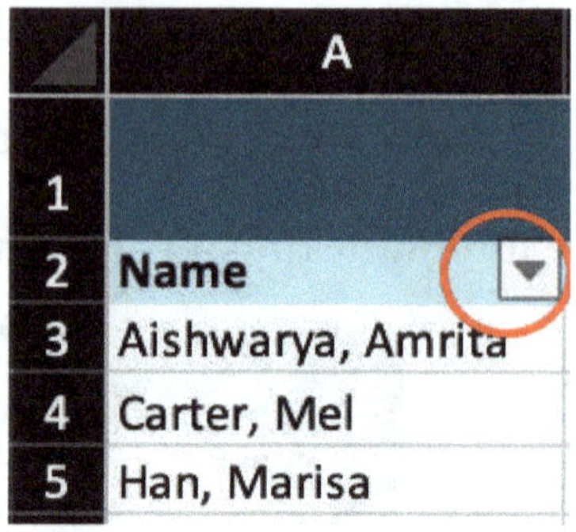

1. Click the down arrow on the <u>Name</u> tab (screenshot on the right).
2. In the drop-down window, click the tick box next to <u>(Select All)</u> to make it unchecked (see screenshot below on the left).
3. Click on any name on the list, then click <u>Apply Filter.</u>
4. You can also scroll to find the name you are looking for.
5. Or you can type the name into the search bar.

After clicking on "Apply Filter" the only name showing on your Stakeholder List should be the name that you chose, along with all the related information located in the other cells.

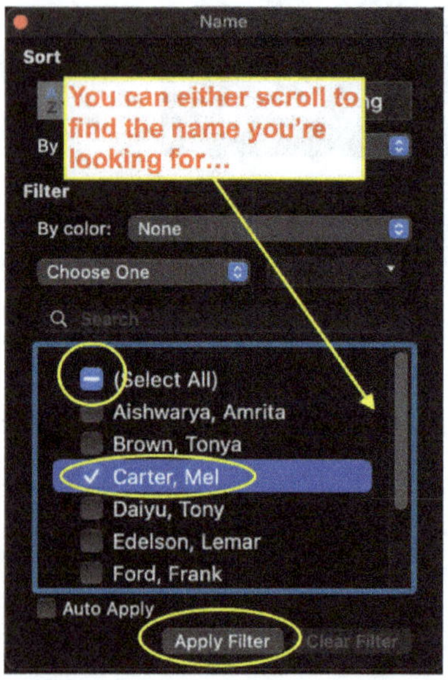

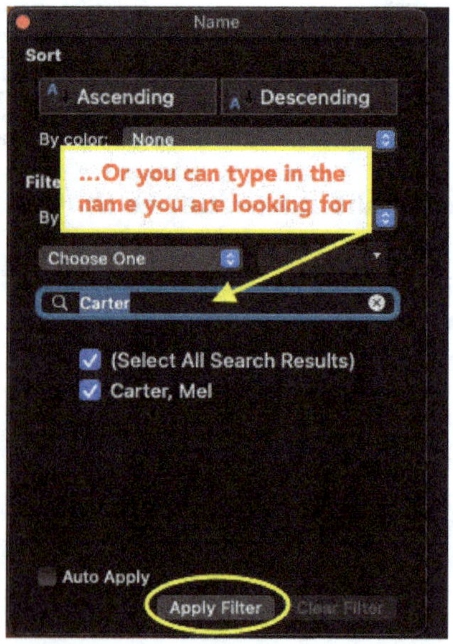

1. Click the down arrow in A2 again (Name), and in the drop-down window, click Clear Filter.

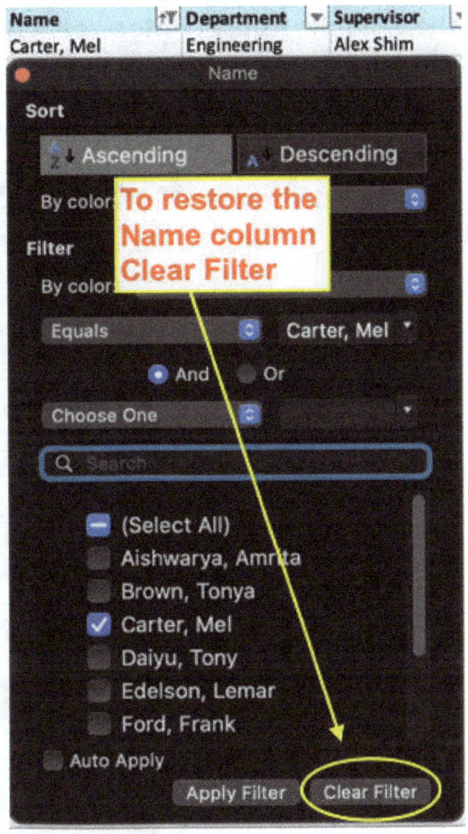

This will restore the list to its unfiltered state.

2. Now click the down arrow next to the Department category (see screenshot on the right).

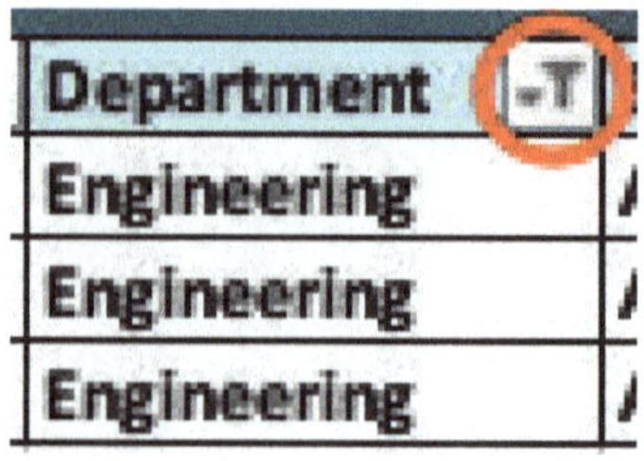

3. In the drop-down window (see below), click Select All to deselect, and then click the box next to Engineering, and then click Apply Filter, or click outside of the drop-down.

The Stakeholder List will show only the staff in the engineering department. Look for the tiny filter symbol (a funnel shape) next to the Department header. This symbol shows which column has been filtered.

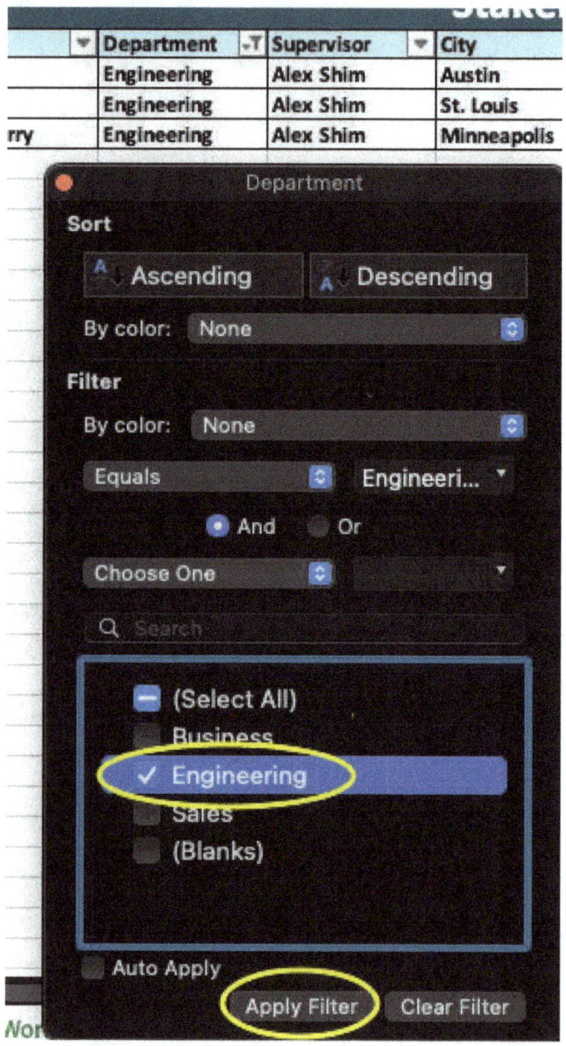

4. Clear the filter.

1. Now click the down-arrow next to Team A.

2. In the pop-up, deselect (Select All) and click the box next to the x. Click Apply Filter.

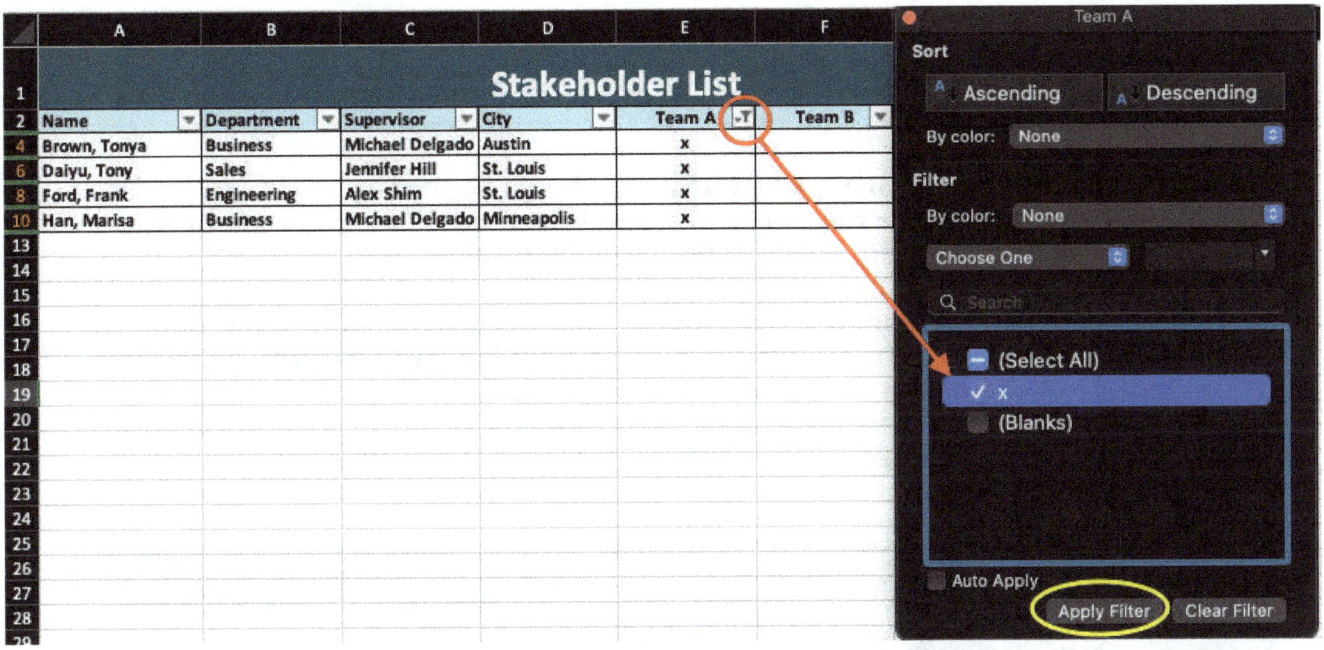

Now the only staff you see are the ones on Team A. The staff on Team B are hidden. That's how the x's work.

Experiment with the filter and sort tools to understand how they function. The filter tool removes all information except that relating to the filter term. The sort tool organizes the information in a specific order.

Apply Alternating Shades to Rows

When looking at a wall of data, it helps to have a shaded color for alternating rows. This makes it easier to visually sort out information.

1. Make sure all the filters are cleared. The Name column should be alphabetically sorted.

2. Select the entire table except for the top header. From A2—G11. (click and drag to select).

Tip: When selecting a table, the top row selected should be the row of categories for each column. If there is a title row above it, as there is on this table, you want to leave that out because that will confuse Excel's formatting functions.

3. Click the Insert tab on the Excel menu. In the Tables section of the ribbon, click the Table tab. To the right and just below the Table tab you will see a section of alternating shaded row options. Select one.

4. To undo, select the table data, click the Table tab, and select the first option to clear the shading.

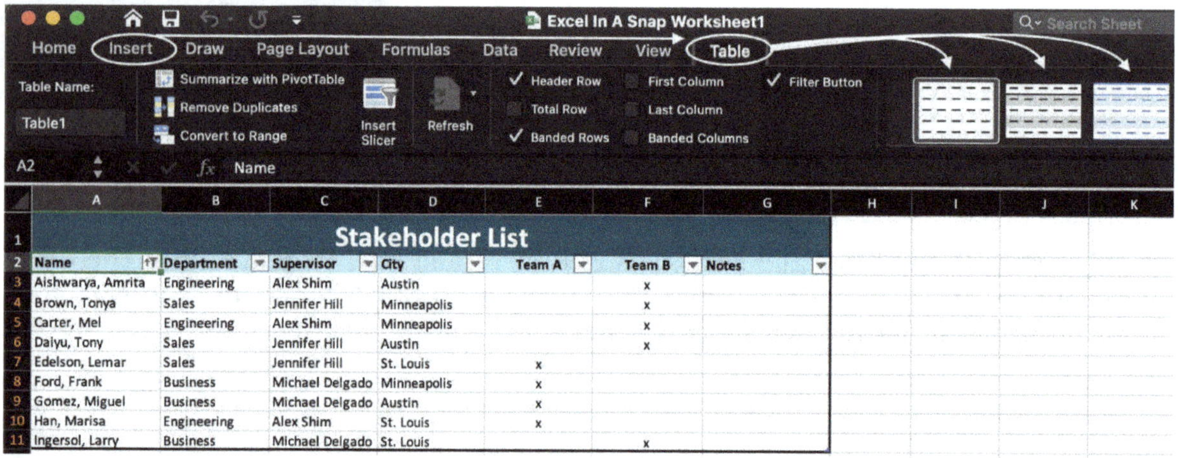

There is another way to add alternating shaded rows to a table that provides more options.

1. Click the Home tab and in the styles section of the ribbon, look for the Format as Table symbol.

2. When you click on the down-arrow a window opens with a gallery of table styles and colors.

3. **Select any of the shading options to apply the table.**

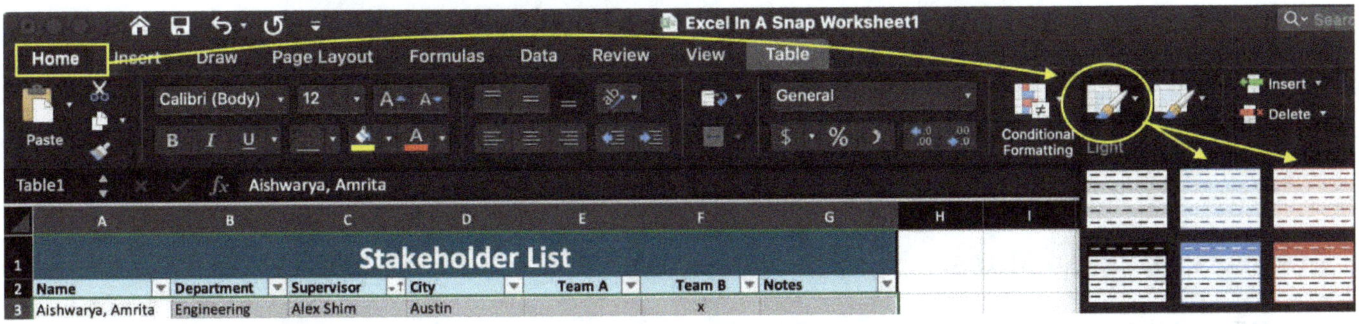

I selected the first table shading option—gray and white. See below. Feel free to play around with this tool.

	A	B	C	D	E	F	G
1	Stakeholder List						
2	Name	Department	Supervisor	City	Team A	Team B	Notes
3	Aishwarya, Amrita	Sales	Jennifer Hill	Austin		x	
4	Brown, Tonya	Business	Michael Delgado	Austin	x		
5	Carter, Mel	Engineering	Alex Shim	Austin		x	
6	Daiyu, Tony	Sales	Jennifer Hill	St. Louis	x		
7	Edelson, Lemar	Business	Michael Delgado	St. Louis		x	
8	Ford, Frank	Engineering	Alex Shim	St. Louis	x		
9	Gomez, Miguel	Sales	Jennifer Hill	Minneapolis		x	
10	Han, Marisa	Business	Michael Delgado	Minneapolis	x		
11	Ingersol, Larry	Engineering	Alex Shim	Minneapolis		x	

Freeze Panes

If this Stakeholder List was tracking a project at a large company, there would likely be well over 100 entries. That means when you scroll down you will quickly lose sight of the category row along with that essential information. But we can freeze the category row so that you can see it no matter how far down you scroll.

Freeze Panes On Macs

Tip: When freezing a row or a column, always select the row *just beneath* the row you want to freeze, or the column *directly to the right* of the column you want to freeze.

1. **Select row 3 by clicking on the header bar for that row (the number 3). See below.**

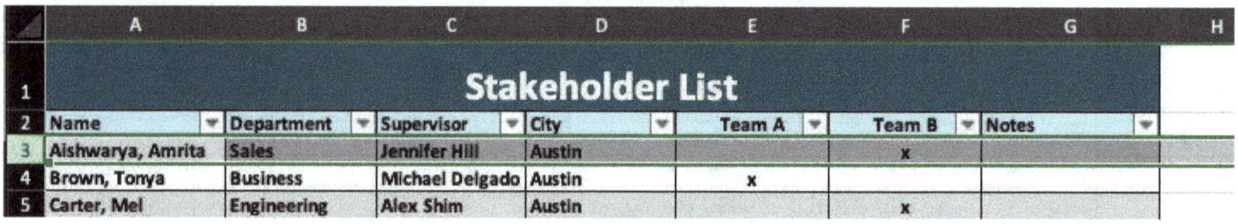

2. **On the App Menu Bar—at the very top of your computer screen—click <u>Window</u> and then <u>Freeze Panes</u>. (See below, right)**

Scroll down on your table. Notice that the content in rows 1 and 2 stays in place while you scroll.

3. **Select Row 3, click <u>Window</u> and <u>Unfreeze Panes</u> to undo it.**

Now we're going to freeze the <u>Name</u> column.

4. **Hover your pointer over the 'B' for Column B (see screenshot on facing page) until it turns into a downward arrow and click to select.**

5. **On the App Menu Bar, click on <u>WindowàFreeze Panes</u>.**

Scroll to the right and you will find that column A stays in place.

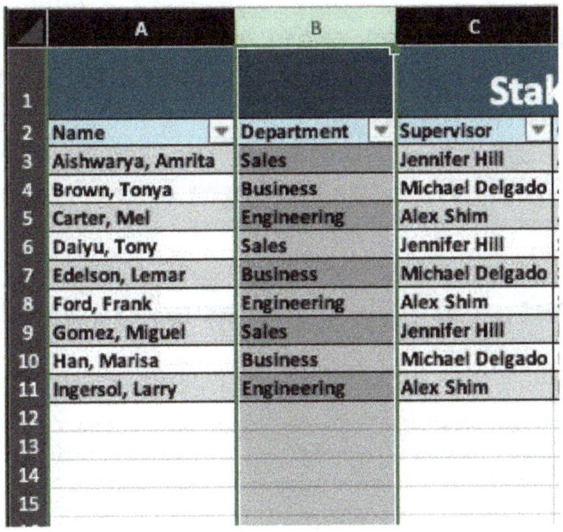

1. **To undo, select Column B.**
2. **Click Window > Unfreeze Panes.**

Now let's freeze both the category row and the Name column.

1. **To freeze both columns and rows at the same time, select the single cell that is directly beneath the row you want to freeze, and directly to the right of the columns.**
2. **Select cell B3.**
3. **On the App Menu Bar, WindowsàFreeze Panes.**

Now, when you scroll up and down, left and right, you will find the category row and the Name column remain in place.

Freeze Panes On Windows

1. **To freeze the category row, select the row just beneath it. This may be either Row 3 or 4, depending on whether the filter function automatically added a column row in Row 2.**

2. **On the Taskbar, click View (to the right of the Home tab), then click Freeze Panes.**

3. **To unfreeze panes, just follow the same click path and choose Unfreeze Panes.**

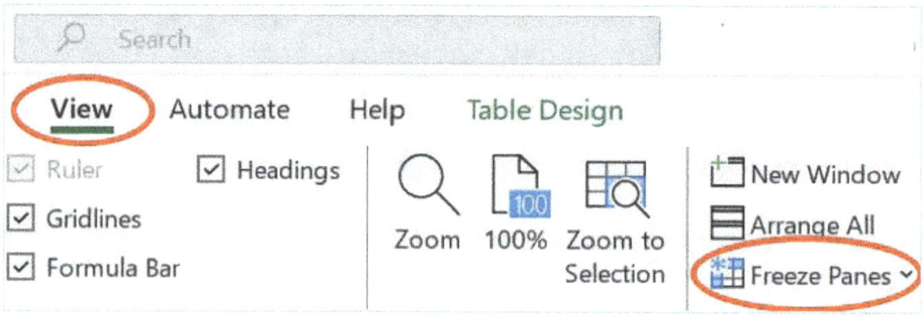

Tip: If the top row, Row 1, is the only row that you want to freeze, you can just choose Freeze Top Row. But that won't work in this case since the top row is just a title.

1. **To freeze Column A, you don't have to choose a column, you can just choose Freeze First Column.**

2. **However, if you want to freeze Column A and B, you need to select Column C, and then click ViewàFreeze Panes.**

3. **To freeze both the category row and the Name column, select the single cell beneath the category row and to the right of the Name column. This will be either cell B3 or B4 depending on whether Row 2 is a column row.**

4. **Click View□Freeze Panes.**

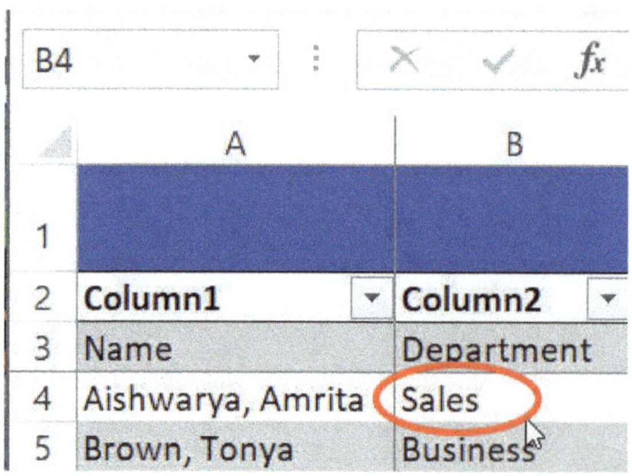

Hide Rows and Columns

Sometimes, as stakeholder lists evolve, they can track so much information that you might want to hide some less important columns or rows so the more important information is easily accessible. Excel makes this possible with the hide tool.

There is a long way to do this, and a quick way. We will do both. Let's start by hiding Rows 6, 7, and 8 the easy way.

Hide and Unhide Rows with Right-Click

1. Hover your pointer over row 6 in the row number bar, until it becomes a right-facing arrow.
2. Click to select and drag down to Row 8 (see image on right).
3. Right-click on the selected rows.
4. In the drop-down menu, click Hide.

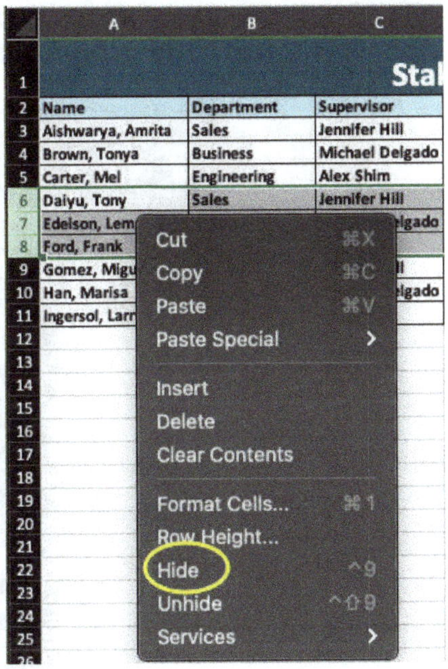

Look at the border between Row 5 and Row 9 (below right). That thick green bar is an indication of the hidden rows.

To unhide the rows:

1. Select rows 5 and 9.
2. Right-click, and select Unhide from the drop-down menu.

Hide and Unhide Rows Using the Ribbon

1. **As before, select rows 6, 7, and 8.**
2. **On the Excel menu, with the Home tab selected, look for Format in the Cells section of the ribbon (a small white box with a tiny blue square - see screenshot below). You may need to expand the window to see it.**
3. **Click the down-arrow next to the Format symbol, select Hide & UnhideàHide Rows from the drop-down menu.**

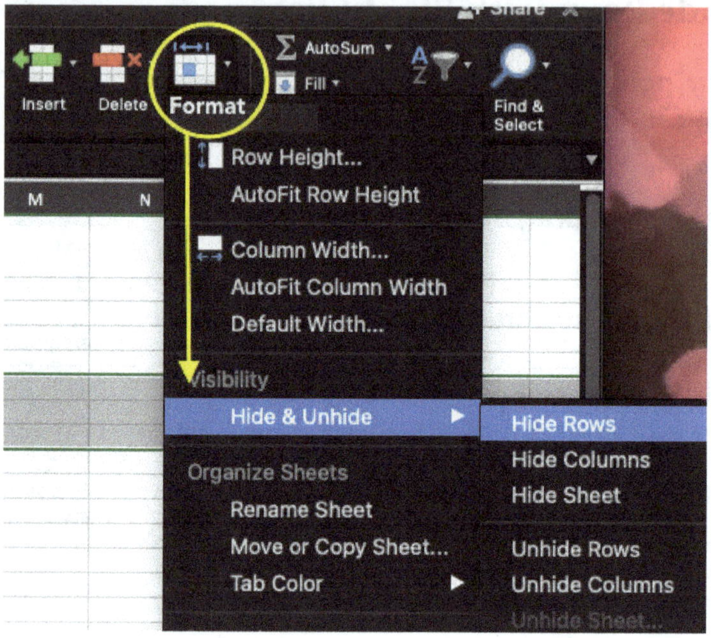

Follow the same instructions to hide columns, after selecting the columns you want to hide.

Excel Formulas

The very reason Excel was invented was to make spreadsheets and mathematical formulas easy to set up and execute. While it is possible to create advanced mathematical formulas—the type you'd find in a trigonometry or linear algebra textbook—we will stick to basic business math since that is what most Excel users employ.

The following table shows basic mathematical equations and how they are written out in the Excel Formula Bar.

Arithmetic Operator	Meaning	Example
+ (plus sign)	Addition	=3+3
- (minus sign)	Subtraction	=3-3
	Negation	=-3
* (asterisk)	Multiplication	=3*3
/ (forward slash)	Division	=3/3
% (percent sign)	Percent	33%
^ (caret)	Exponentiation	=3^3

Tip: The reason all formulas start with an = sign is because that signals to Excel that the cell contains a formula. Without it, Excel sees the cell content as data.

Reference Operator	Meaning	Example
: (colon)	Range operator; this defines a range of cells, usually filled with numbers and/or formulas	B5:B15 This configuration is like highlighting a column of cells made up of B5 through B15
, (comma)	Union operator, generally functions to add or combine ranges of numbers	=SUM(B5:B15,D5:D15) This formula instructs Excel to add the sum of the numerical values in cells B5 through B15, to the sum of the numerical

	values in D5 through D15

Mathematical Order of Operations

It's important to follow the order of operations when creating formulas in Excel to get accurate results. Here is an explanation of how Excel will calculate a simple equation like the one below.

=10 + (6-2) / 2^2

When Excel calculates formulas, it uses the mathematical order of operations which are outlined below.

Parenthesis

Calculations within parenthesis are performed first. Once you subtract 2 from 6, the equation is:

=10 + 4/2^2

Exponents

Exponents are performed next. Once we determine 2 to the power of 2 by multiplying 2 by itself we get 4. Now the equation is:

=10+4/4

Multiplication and Division

Multiplication and division are performed next, whichever comes first in the equation. Once we divide 4 by 4, the equation is:

=10 +1

Addition and Subtraction

Addition and subtraction are performed next, whichever comes first. Once we add 10 to 1, we get:

=11

If you do the math out of order you can get a variety of results, but only this one is accurate.

PROJECT 2: Grocery Budget

Our first formula project will be a simple grocery budget. If you've downloaded the Excel In A Snap Project Worksheets file, click on the sheet <u>2. Grocery Budget</u>. *Reminder: You can find the project file on INaSnapGuides.com.*

Otherwise, create a new sheet by clicking on the plus (+) symbol next to the worksheet tab, title it "Grocery Budget" and fill it out as shown on the right.

	A	B	C
1	Household Monthly Grocery Budget For July		
2	Grocery budget	300	
3	Gig Income	50	
4	Total Grocery Budget		
5	Unspent funds	30	
6	Total Grocery $ Spent		
7	Divided by 3 Roommates		

In this project, we will format the header to reinforce those skills. See if you can format the header by memory.

Tip: The more you use these skills, the more easily you'll remember them in the future. Your brain lays down memory pathways that get stronger and stronger with each repetition of various tasks.

1. **Format the header reminder: Merge cells A1 through C1. Then, with the Home tab selected, use the Font and Paint-bucket tools in the ribbon to adjust the colors and text size.**
2. **To enter two or more lines in a single cell, click into the cell, then click into the Formula Bar and place your pointer where you want the line to break.**
3. **Press <u>Option</u> + <u>Control</u> (or <u>Alt</u> on Windows) on your keyboard and hit <u>Return/Enter</u>.**

	A	B	C
1	Household Monthly Grocery Budget For July		
2	Grocery budget	$ 300.00	
3	Gig Income	$ 50.00	
4	Total Grocery Budget		
5	Unspent funds	$ 30.00	
6	Total Grocery $ Spent		
7	Divided by 3 Roommates		
8			

Turn Numbers Into Dollar Values

1. Select column B.

2. With the Home tab selected, in the Number section of the ribbon, look for the dollar sign symbol ($) and click the down arrow next to it.

3. From the drop-down window, click on $ English (United States) (see below).

4. If Excel is not full screen, the program may display the ribbon's sections as symbols. In this situation, look for the large % sign and click the down arrow next to it. Next, click the down arrow next to the dollar sign and select $ English (United States) as shown below.

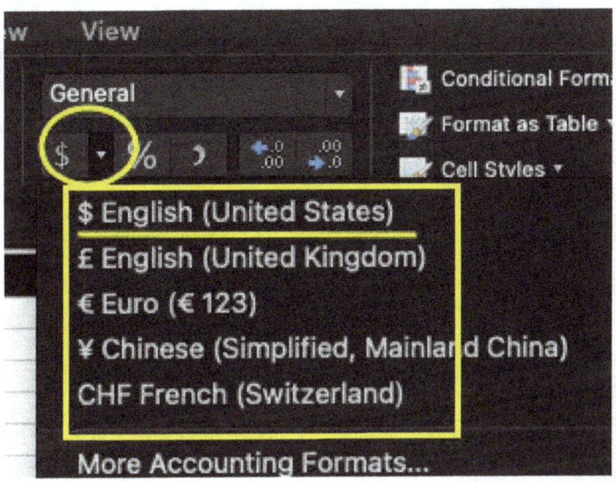

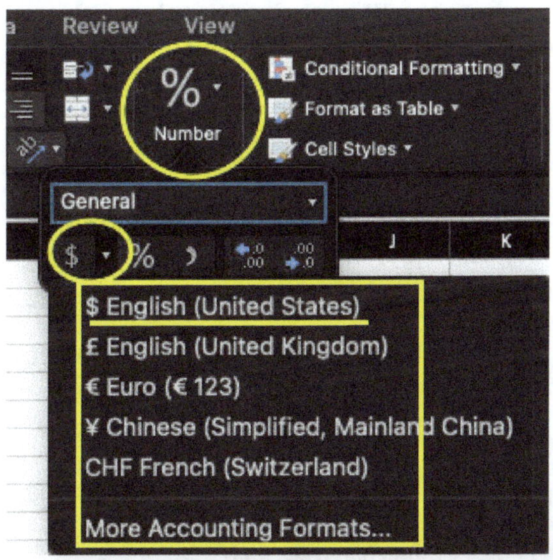

5. Fill in cell B4 with the formula =SUM(B2+B3)

6. Fill in cell B6 with the formula =SUM(B4-B5)

7. Fill in cell B7 with the formula =SUM(B6/3)

Notice that cell B6 contains a number but the formula bar contains the formula that produced that number.

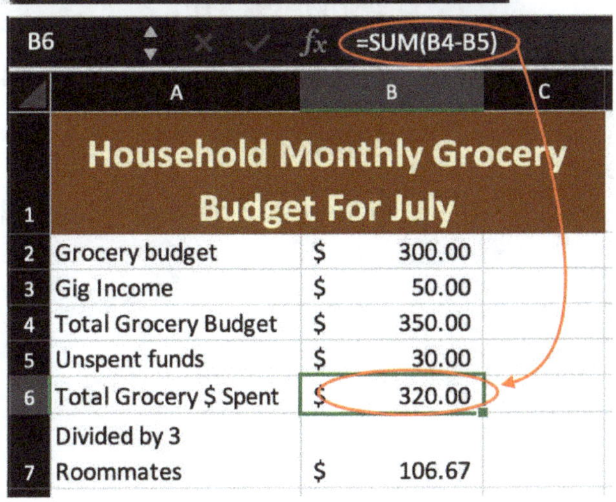

PROJECT 3: Shopping List

Our next formula project will be a shopping list for a painting project. First, we will add up all the items to get a subtotal, subtract the 15%-off coupon, calculate the sales tax, the total, and then we will divide the total into four payments. This will require formulas for addition, subtraction, multiplication, and division.

If you have the *Excel In A Snap Project Worksheets* file, go to the 3. Paint Project tab. If not, then recreate the table shown below on a new sheet.

Fill in the numbers and then turn them into dollar values all at once as shown in the prior exercise.

Using Formulas In Your Shopping List

Let's fill in the rest of the table.

	A	B
1	**Shopping List for Paint Project**	
2	tape	$ 7.00
3	rollers	$ 16.50
4	crown molding	$ 120.00
5	roller handles	$ 20.00
6	paint	$ 85.00
7	paint pans	$ 18.00
8	**Subtotal**	
9	**Subtotal minus 15% off**	
10	7.5% tax	
11	**Total**	
12	4 monthly payments of:	

1. **In cell B8 enter the formula**

   =SUM(B2:B7)

2. **In cell B9 enter the formula**

   =B8-(B8*0.15)

3. **In cell B10 enter the formula**

   =(B9*0.075)

4. **In cell B11 enter the formula**

   =SUM(B9+B10)

5. **In cell B12 enter the formula**

   =B11/4

6. **When you have finished filling in the formulas, add the dollar signs.**

Your table should look like the one below. For your convenience, the formulas are shown in blue next to the numerical values that they produce.

	A	B	C
1	**Shopping List for Paint Project**		
2	tape	$ 7.00	
3	rollers	$ 16.50	
4	crown molding	$ 120.00	
5	roller handles	$ 20.00	
6	paint	$ 85.00	
7	paint pans	$ 18.00	
8	**Subtotal**	**$ 266.50**	=SUM(B2:B7)
9	**Subtotal minus 15% off**	**$ 226.53**	=B8-(B8*.15)
10	7.5% tax	$ 16.99	=(B9*0.075)
11	**Total**	**$ 243.51**	=SUM(B9+B10)
12	4 monthly payments of:	$ 60.88	=B11/4

Let's walk through the basic math to see how we arrived at these formulas.

B8 =SUM(B2:B7) This sums up the price of all the items on the list to calculate the subtotal.

B9 =B8-(B8*0.15) This subtracts the 15 percent discount coupon from the subtotal. The 15 percent discount is calculated by multiplying the subtotal by 0.15.

B10 =(B9*0.075) This formula calculates the sales tax by multiplying the new subtotal by 0.075 which is 7.5 percent.

B11 =SUM(B9+B10) This adds the tax to the final subtotal to create the Total.

B12 =B11/4 This divides the Total into four monthly payments.

PROJECT 4: Mortgage Calculator

It's easy to find a mortgage calculator online. But creating your own is a great way to practice your budding Excel formula skills. Fortunately, most mortgage formulas are just basic math a 5th grader would understand. For this exercise, you can either go to the *Excel In A Snap Project Worksheets* file and click on the tab 4. Mortgage Calculator, or create a new worksheet and fill in your own values.

Setting Up Your Mortgage Calculator

To create a new worksheet, click the plus (+) symbol next to the worksheet tabs at the bottom of the window, and double click on the tab to name it "Mortgage Calculator"

1. **In cell A-1, type the header "Calculate Mortgage Principal and Interest" and in cells A-2 through A-9 type the following terms. Use the graphic to the right as a guide.**

2. **Cell A2**

   House Price

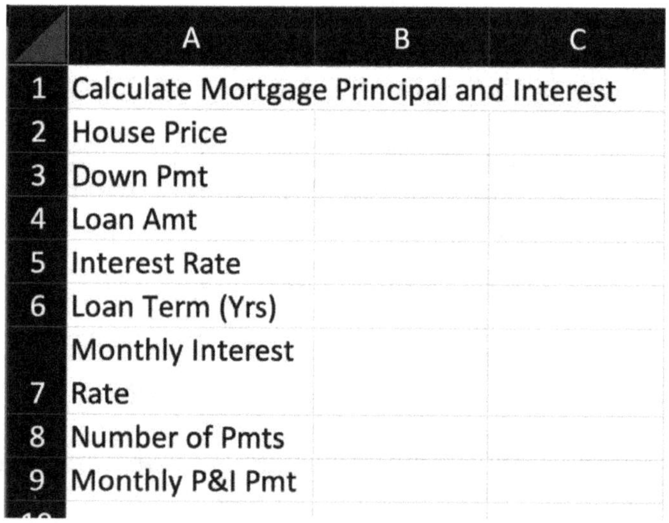

3. **Cell A3**

   Down Pmt

4. **Cell A4**

   Loan Amt

5. **Cell A5**

   Interest Rate

6. **Cell A6**

   Loan Term (Yrs)

7. **Cell A7**

   Monthly Interest Rate

8. **Cell A8**

   Number of Pmts

9. **Cell A9**

   Monthly P&I Pmt

Notice that several of the cells overlap into column B. You can ignore the top header row and just widen the column to accommodate the entries below the header.

1. **Widen Column A.**
2. **Format Header Row: Select cells A-1 through C-1.**
3. **With the Home tab selected in the Excel menu, click the Merge and Center symbol in the Alignment section of the ribbon. (See below)**

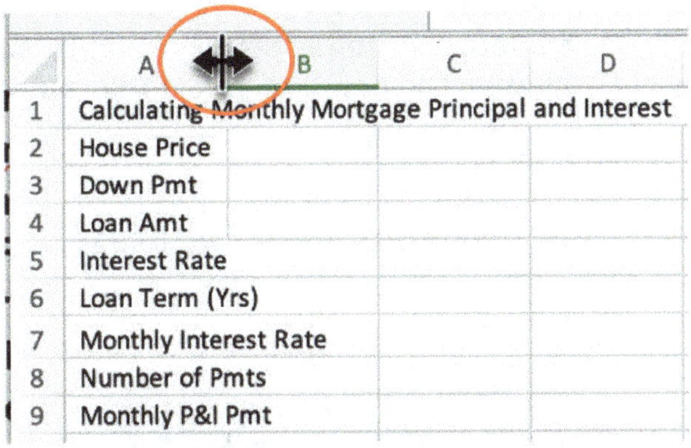

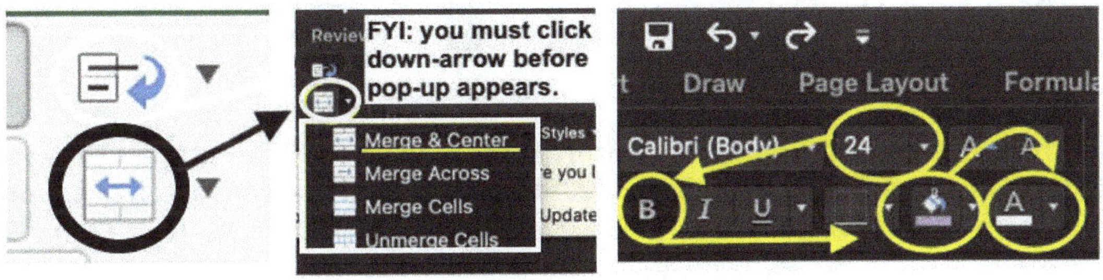

4. **With the Header row still selected, change the font size to 24, Bold the text, color-fill the cell with a dark color, and change the text to white.**

If you cannot see all the text in the header, hover your pointer over the horizontal line between the row numbers '1' and '2', wait for the double arrow, then click and drag down until row 1 is tall enough that you can see all of the text. The screenshot in the upper right of the facing page shows the full header after you expand row 1.

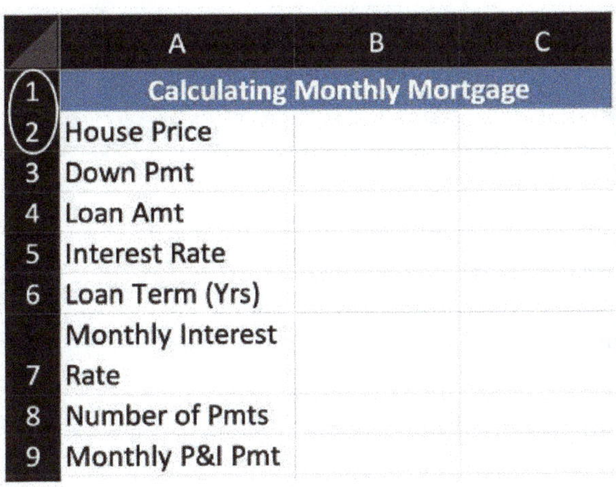

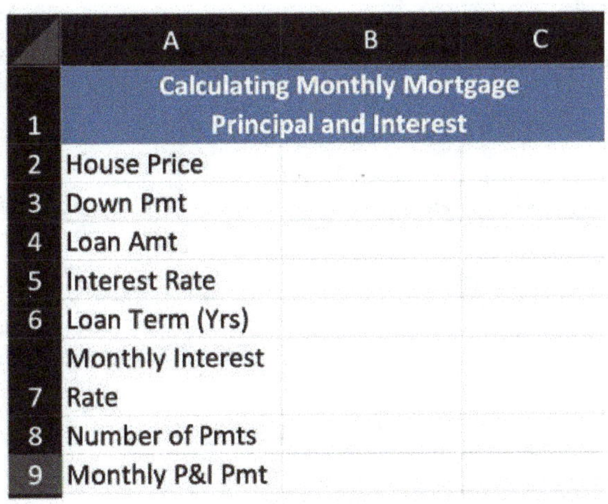

Fill out column B with the following data:

1. **Cell B2**

   300,000
   (Select the dollar sign symbol in the number section of the Home ribbon to change the figure to a US dollar amount)

2. **Cell B3**

   60,000 (Add a dollar sign to B3)

3. **Cell B5**

   6.5 (Leave as is)

4. **B6**

   30

	A	B	C
1	Calculating Monthly Mortgage Principal and Interest		
2	House Price	$ 300,000.00	
3	Down Pmt	$ 60,000.00	
4	Loan Amt		
5	Interest Rate	6.5	
6	Loan Term (Yrs)	30	
7	Monthly Interest Rate		
8	Number of Pmts		
9	Monthly P&I Pmt		

While the number in B5 signifies an interest rate, do not add an interest rate symbol as that will dramatically change the value. This number will be converted to an interest rate in an upcoming formula.

The value in B6 is the loan term in years.

When you're done, your worksheet should look like the one above.

Now we will fill in the formulas to calculate the loan amount (B4), the monthly interest rate (B5), the number of payments (B8), and the monthly principle and interest payment (B9).

1. **Cell B4**

   =B2-B3

2. **Cell B7**

   =B5/12/100

3. **Cell B8**

   =B6*12

4. **Fill in cell B9 with this Mortgage formula:**

   =PMT(B7,B8,-B4)

5. **Change the Monthly Interest Rate (B7) to a percentage figure.**

   a. **With cell B7 selected, click on the percentage sign (%) in the Number section of the Home ribbon (next to the $ sign).**

   b. **If you get a number 1, click the "Decrease Decimal" button (the circled button below on the right) arrow twice to move the decimal point to the left.**

Once you have filled in all of the formulas, your table should have the same figures as shown below.

If your workbook looks different, double-check the amounts and formulas entered in the previous step

Save this Mortgage Calculator. We will use some of these figures in the Amortization Table in Project 5, and for a pie chart in Project 6.

	A	B	C
1	Calculating Monthly Mortgage Principal and Interest		
2	House Price	300,000	
3	Down Pmt	60,000	
4	Loan Amt	240,000	
5	Interest Rate	6.5	
6	Loan Term (Yrs)	30	
7	Monthly Interest Rate	0.54%	
8	Number of Pmts	360	
9	Monthly P&I Pmt	$ 1,516.96	

PROJECT 5: Amortization Table

Now we will build an Amortization Table directly beneath the Mortgage Calculator starting on Row 10.

If you have the downloaded project worksheet file, select tab 5. Amortization Table. Use the arrows on the far left to scroll right if necessary.

Reminder: You can find the downloadable file Excel In A Snap Project Worksheets on INaSnapGuides.com

Otherwise, start your Amortization Table just beneath your Mortgage Calculator as shown below.

It's helpful to have the Mortgage Calculator just above the Amortization Table since crucial data is drawn from the former to be used in the latter. Before we start, please know this will be a very long table since we will calculate the principal and interest for every single payment of the loan.

	A	B	C	D	E	F	G
1	Calculating Monthly Mortgage Principal and Interest						
2	House Price	300,000					
3	Down Pmt	60,000					
4	Loan Amt	240,000					
5	Interest Rate	6.5					
6	Loan Term (Yrs)	30					
7	Monthly Interest Rate	0.54%					
8	Number of Pmts	360					
9	Monthly P&I Pmt	$ 1,516.96					
10	Payment Number	Payment Date	Beginning Balance	Scheduled Payment	Principal	Interest	Ending Balance
11	1	1/1/25					

With your typical 30-year fixed loan, if the home buyer pays until the end of the loan term, there will be 360 monthly payments in all. That is 12 months x 30 years = 360 payments. So, when you build out the payment column, you will take the column 360 rows down. Since you are starting on row A11, the final row will be Row 370, not 360.

At the end of this lesson, the ending balance in cell G370 should be $0.00.

Once you've established the bottom row, you can send all of the other formulas down to the bottom of the table with one double-click. That's coming up.

Keep in mind, most of these formulas will not calculate accurately until all of the relevant cells have been filled in with either numbers or formulas. So please don't judge your work until the entire table is filled in.

Some cells may contain a line of hashtags, like #####. This means the number in that cell cannot be displayed because the width of the cell is too narrow. Simply widen that column using the techniques you learned in previous lessons. If the hashtags remain, there's likely another issue., such as dates and times with negative values.

If you have trouble getting the formulas to display the intended output, double-check your work to make sure you have the right formulas in the right cells. If it still doesn't work after adjustments are made, you can copy and paste the Mortgage Calculator table and just the header row of the Amortization Table to a new sheet and start over.

Let's build out this table.

The first thing to do is format row 10, which includes expanding its height to make room for a text box that will contain the title: Amortization Table.

Create Your Amortization Table

1. To format the Amortization Table header, select rows A10 through G10. Do NOT merge the cells. We need to keep the column headers in row 10 intact so Excel can read them.

   Use the Paint Bucket tool to color fill the cells' background to the same dark color as the Mortgage Calculator header above it.

   Use the font color tool (the letter 'A' symbol just right of the Paint Bucket) to change the font color to white.

2. To make room for a text box that will contain the Amortization Table's title, hover the pointer in the row number bar on the far left of the worksheet, between rows 10 and 11, until you see the double arrow. Then click and drag down to increase the height of Row 10. (See screenshot at bottom of facing page.)

Add a Text Box

We will add the title "Amortization Table" to the header without placing it on a separate row to avoid misalignment of numbers. The first mortgage payment should align with row 11 for simplicity. Follow the instructions below to place the title in a text box and color-fill it with a lighter shade of the color of the header.

1. Click somewhere inside the header row.

2. **Click Insert in the Excel menu (to the right of the Home tab).**

3. **In the Text section of the ribbon, select the white square with the letter "A" in the upper left. Click on this icon to enable the text box drawing feature.**

4. **If the Excel window is too narrow, the Text section may be depicted as a tilted blue "A". Click the downward arrow and then select the Text Box icon.**

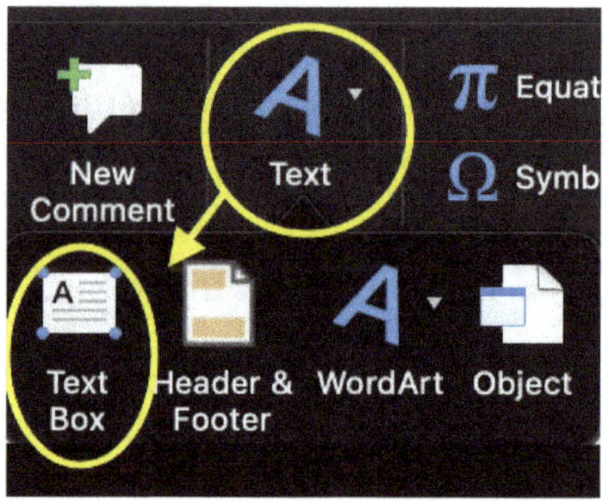

5. **Your pointer will change to an arrow with a black square containing an uppercase A. When you click in the upper middle of Row 10 of the worksheet, a text box will be drawn at that location.**

6. **Click and drag to draw a text box in the middle of the header in row 10.**

7. **In the text box type, "AMORTIZATION TABLE".**

8. **Click on the Home tab and use the font tools in the ribbon to increase the text size and choose a text color.**

9. **Use the Paint Bucket tool to color-fill your text box.**

   To reposition the Text Box, hover the pointer over the text box's border until it turns into a plus sign with arrows at each end (you might have to move the pointer around a bit before the plus sign shows up). Click-and-hold to drag the text box into place.

It's a good idea to choose a pale shade of the header's background color. Or you can make the title text white with no background, like the column headings.

When you're done, the new header should look like the one below. Make the columns wider as needed.

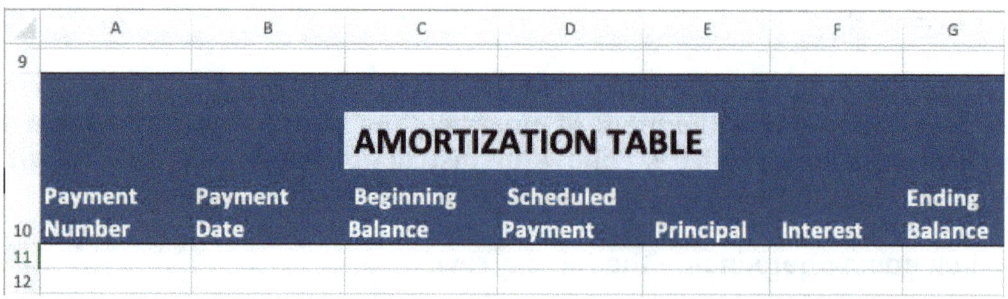

Let's fill in the figures and formulas. It's a good idea to take this slowly.

Tip: As you enter figures and formulas into each individual cell, it's a good idea to keep your eye on the Cell Address Box to make sure you're entering the desired content into the correct cell.

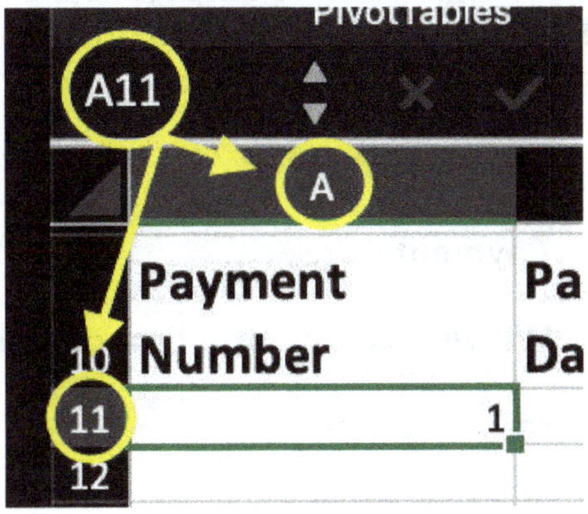

Before we go further, we need to format several cells for dollar amounts.

When we do that ahead of time, that formatting will be in place when we send these formulas down to Row 370.

Input Amortization Figures and Formulas

1. Select cells C11 through G11.
2. On the Home tab, and in the Number section of the Ribbon, click the down-arrow next to the dollar sign ($), and select <u>$ English (United States).</u>

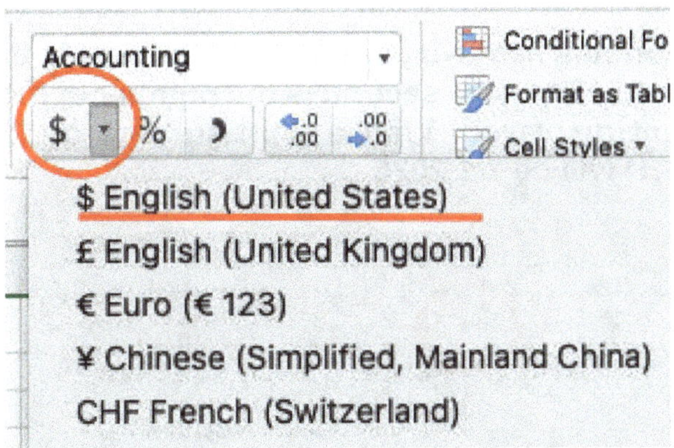

Create a Column of Consecutive Numbers

1. In cell A11, enter the numeral 1.
2. In cell A12, enter the formula:

   =A11+1

3. **With just A12 selected, hover your pointer over the small square in the lower right of the cell until you see the plus sign, then click and drag the cell down to row 370 (be patient, it's a long journey…don't go too fast!)**

These consecutive numbers represent the total of 360 payments over the loan term of 30 years. When you are finished with this step, the cells in column A, from A11 through A370, should be numbered consecutively from 1 - 360.

4. **In Cell B10 enter:**

   Payment Date

   We will assume the first payment date is Jan. 1, 2025.

5. **In B11, enter**

   1/1/2025

6. **In B12, enter the formula:**

   =EDATE(B11,1)

7. **If you get a number instead of a date, make sure you are on the Home tab and cell B12 is still selected.**

8. **Go to the Taskbar and in the cell formatting section (see below—the text field should show "General"), click the down-arrow, and then click Short Date.**

9. **The EDATE formula has two parameters. The first is the starting date, which you referenced in B11. The second is the number of months after the starting date you want displayed. With a starting date of 1/1/2025, the output of =EDATE(B11,1) will be 2/1/2025.**

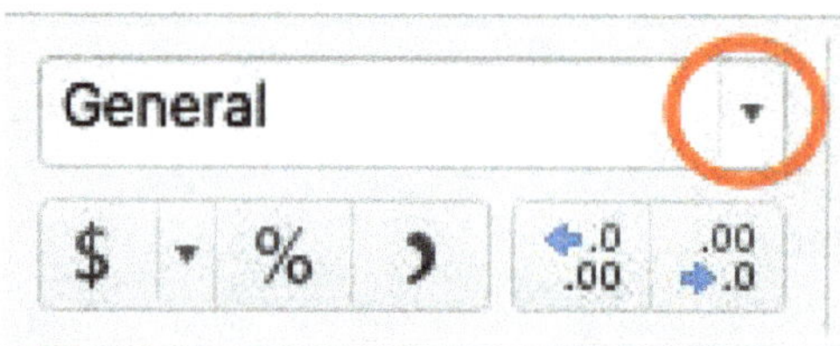

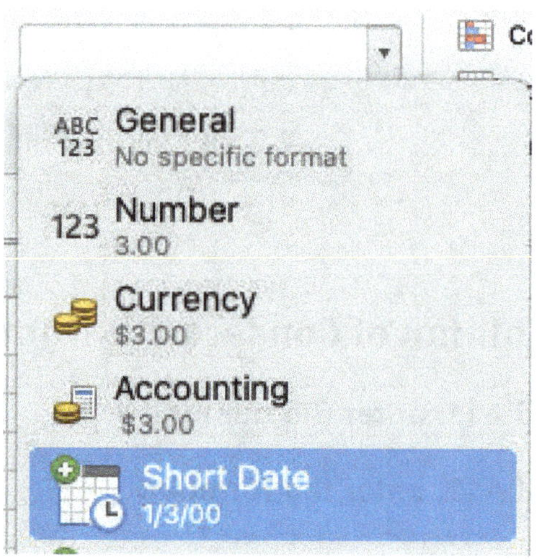

Copy Cell Contents to the Bottom of a Table With Double-Click

Now that we've established the lower boundary of the table, one double-click will copy formulas all the way to the bottom.

To copy the formula in B12 all the way down to B370 in one double-click:

1. Select B11 and B12, hover your pointer over the cell until the pointer becomes a black plus sign, and then double-click to copy the formula into each cell all the way down to B370.

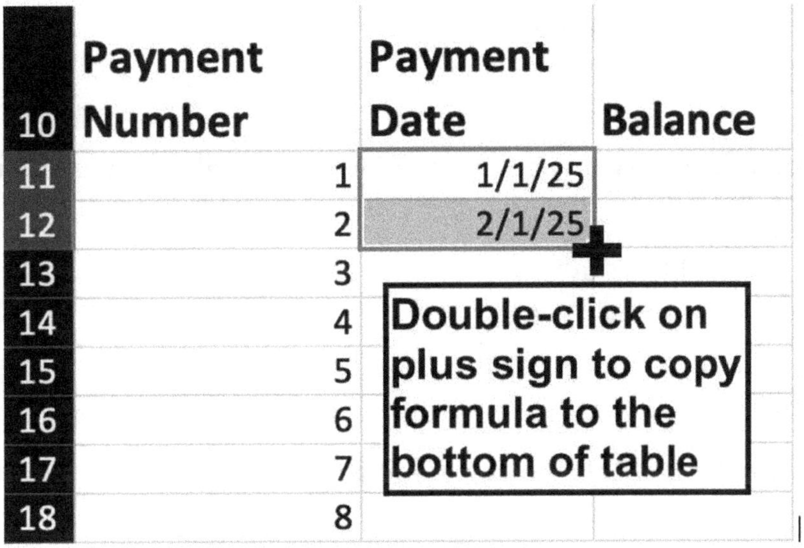

Note: Make sure your pointer is a BLACK plus sign before you double-click. If you double-click when the plus sign is WHITE, you will enter a different editing mode.

2. Click cell B13 and check the formula bar. Notice the formula is =EDATE(B12,1), not =EDATE(B11,1). Excel incremented the output by one month from the cell above. This is called a "relative" reference, using values from cells relative to the cell with the formula.

Entering Absolute References To Calculate The Amortization Chart

1. In cell C11, enter: =$B$4

This is the total loan amount taken from cell B4 in the Mortgage Calculator. The $ signs indicate an Absolute Reference, ensuring that when a formula is copied to another cell, it will reference the original cell. This means if the value of the original cell (the loan amount) is changed, all other cells referencing it will automatically update.

2. In cell C12, enter: =G11

This updates the monthly balance with the ending balance of the prior month after the monthly principal and interest have been subtracted.

3. **Copy this formula down to the bottom of the table by double-clicking on the plus sign of the cell pointer as shown on the prior page.**

Scheduled Payment

1. **In cell D11, enter the formula: (This is the monthly mortgage payment)**

   =$B$9

2. **Copy it down as shown above.**

Interest

(Skipping to cell F11 may seem odd, but the formulas might not pan out unless you do it in this order.)

1. **In cell F11, enter the formula:**

   =C11*$B$7

2. **Copy it down.**

This will calculate the monthly interest for each payment period.

Principal

1. **In cell E11, enter:**

   =D11-F11

2. **Copy it down.**

This formula will calculate the principal payment by subtracting the interest from the total payment.

Ending Balance

1. **In cell G11, enter:**

   =C11-E11

2. **Copy it down.**

This formula subtracts only the principal payment (not the interest) from the previous monthly balance aka the Beginning Balance to create the Ending Balance.

Check Your Work

First, give the computer a minute to fill in all the cells. Column E, Principal, can take some time. See if your numbers match the ones in the screen-capture below.

1. **Scroll to row 370, the bottom of the amortization chart.**
2. **If cell G370 is (0.00) that means you did it right.**

Notice the amount of the principal and the amount of the interest is updated month by month. This is specifically what makes it an Amortization Table.

AMORTIZATION TABLE

	A	B	C	D	E	F	G
10	Payment Number	Payment Date	Beginning Balance	Scheduled Payment	Principal	Interest	Ending Balance
11	1	1/1/25	$ 240,000.00	$ 1,516.96	$ 216.96	$ 1,300.00	$ 239,783.04
12	2	2/1/25	$ 239,783.04	$ 1,516.96	$ 218.14	$ 1,298.82	$ 239,564.90
13	3	3/1/25	$ 239,564.90	$ 1,516.96	$ 219.32	$ 1,297.64	$ 239,345.58
14	4	4/1/25	$ 239,345.58	$ 1,516.96	$ 220.51	$ 1,296.46	$ 239,125.07
15	5	5/1/25	$ 239,125.07	$ 1,516.96	$ 221.70	$ 1,295.26	$ 238,903.37
16	6	6/1/25	$ 238,903.37	$ 1,516.96	$ 222.90	$ 1,294.06	$ 238,680.46

	A	B	C	D	E	F	G
368	358	10/1/54	$ 4,502.03	$ 1,516.96	$ 1,492.58	$ 24.39	$ 3,009.45
369	359	11/1/54	$ 3,009.45	$ 1,516.96	$ 1,500.66	$ 16.30	$ 1,508.79
370	360	12/1/54	$ 1,508.79	$ 1,516.96	$ 1,508.79	$ 8.17	$ (0.00)

If the numbers don't pan out as in the screenshot above, double-check all your formulas. Look for any blank cells that might need to be filled in. If you see any columns where the cells are filled with hashtags, try widening the column.

PROJECT 6: Graphs and Charts

Graphs and charts can be a bit fussy, but as you play around with this tool it will become second nature. We will start with a bar chart.

When working with charts, sometimes you get a completely wrong result. For example, you might wind up with a bar chart where all the bars are the exact same height when the data indicates they should be various heights. Or, one set of data might be the Y axis and another set of data the X axis, and you wanted it the other way around. If this happens, delete the chart (but keep the source data intact) and create a new chart. You might have to do this a couple of times before you get the chart you want.

Reminder: Let's take another look at Excel's navigation arrows for the worksheets. Sometimes when you have a lot of sheets some might not be visible.

You can navigate through the sheet tabs using the double, triangular arrows on the bottom left of the Excel window. See screenshot below.

Bar Chart

This will be a chart that compares the PE ratios of well-known companies on the stock market.

1. If you have the downloaded *Excel In A Snap Worksheets* file, select the tab labeled 6. Bar Chart.

2. Otherwise, click the plus sign at the bottom of the Excel window to create a new sheet.

3. Double-click on the new sheet tab to name it "Bar Chart".

4. **Fill out the worksheet with the following data.**

	A	B
1.	Company	PE Ratio
2.	Meta	27.00
3.	Alphabet/Google	24.00
4.	Apple	34.00
5.	Microsoft	35.00
6.	Amazon	42.00
7.	Tesla	62.00
8.	Nvidia	75.00
9.	Average for M-7	=AVERAGE(B2:B8)
10.	GM	5.00
11.	AT&T	11.00
12.	Target	17.00
13.	IBM	21.00

5. **In cell B-9 type the formula:**

   =AVERAGE(B3:B8)

   a. **If the output from this formula displays decimal values more than two places, tap the HOME tab, and in the Number section, click the drop down and select CURRENCY. This will limit the digits behind the decimal point to two.**

This will give you the average PE ratio for each of the first 7 companies.

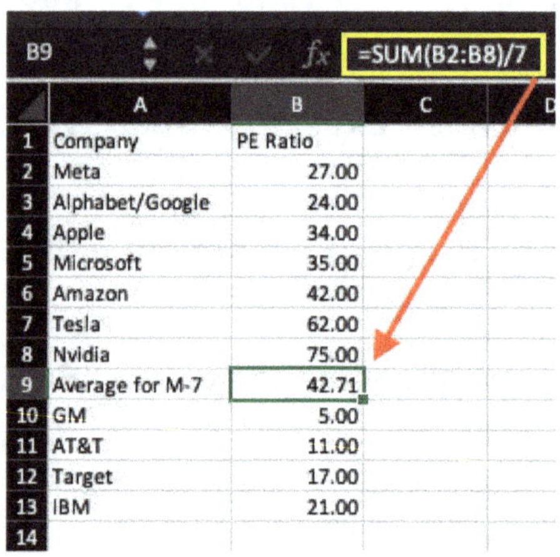

B9 =SUM(B2:B8)/7

	A	B	C
1	Company	PE Ratio	
2	Meta	27.00	
3	Alphabet/Google	24.00	
4	Apple	34.00	
5	Microsoft	35.00	
6	Amazon	42.00	
7	Tesla	62.00	
8	Nvidia	75.00	
9	Average for M-7	42.71	
10	GM	5.00	
11	AT&T	11.00	
12	Target	17.00	
13	IBM	21.00	
14			

6. **Select the entire table from A1 to B13.**

7. Click the Insert tab in the Excel menu (see below).

8. Click the smaller bar chart symbol.

9. Click the box for the 3-D column (or the 2-D if you prefer).

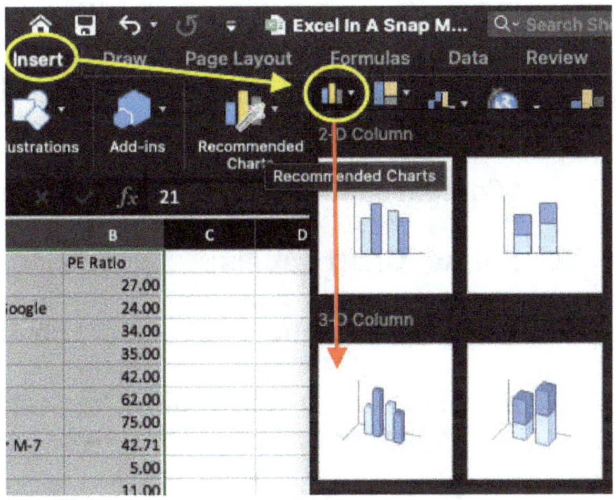

This will bring up a bar chart. Notice that you can move this chart around on the worksheet.

You can also select it and use the square handles on each corner to resize bigger or smaller.

Trouble Shooting: If something is wrong with the chart you can select it, delete it, and start over. But don't touch the data in Column A and B.

You'll know if you generated an accurate chart if it looks like the one below. Now let's format it.

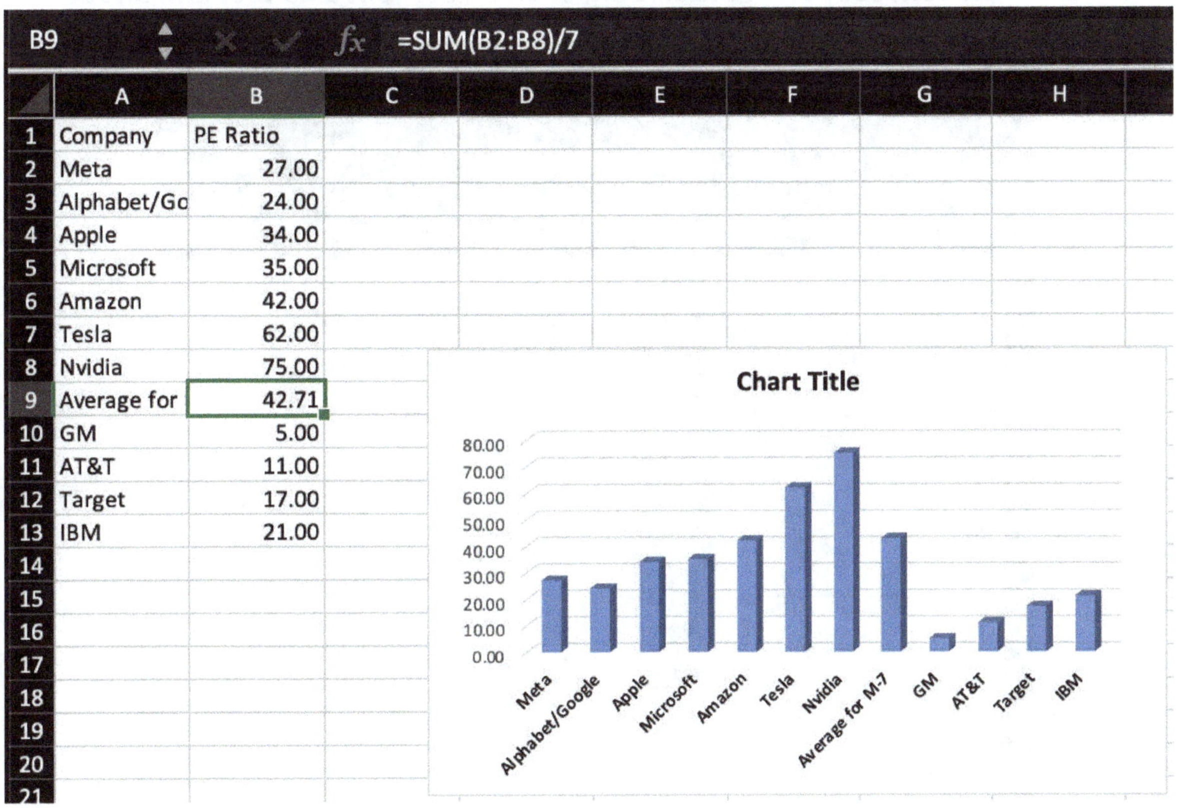

Formatting A Bar Chart

1. **Change Title:**

   a. **Double click on the Chart Title and change it to:**

   "Magnificent 7 P/E Ratios" without the quotes.

   b. **Hit <u>RETURN</u> on Mac or <u>ENTER</u> on Windows, and then in the next row type:**

   "Compared to Conventional Companies" without the quotes.

2. **Format Chart Labels:**

To make the text labels on the bottom either larger or smaller:

   a. **Click in the text region beneath the bars; a square around the text will appear indicating it has been selected.**

   b. **Click the Home tab on the Excel menu.**

   c. **In the font section of the ribbon, click on the font size tool and choose 12.**

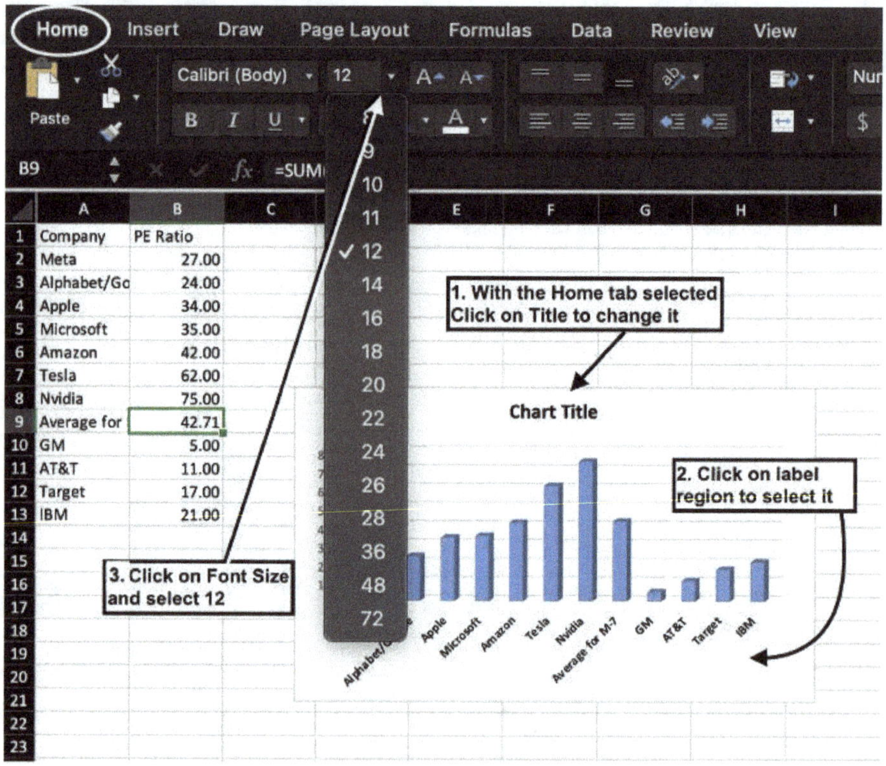

3. **Enlarge Your Chart:**

Tip: If the bars seem crowded after you increase the font size for the bottom labels you can expand the chart window, as follows:

   a. Click on the chart so that a square appears around it indicating it has been selected, then look for the tiny squares, or handles, on each corner and on the sides.

   b. Hover your pointer over one of the handles until it turns into a double-arrow.

   c. Click and drag to size the chart window. If you want to keep the same dimensions, choose a corner.

Next, we're going to change the colors of some of the bars in the chart. We'll keep The Magnificent 7 stocks as blue. And we'll choose gold for the bar corresponding to "Average for M7," and red for the remaining bars.

Formatting Bars Via Format Tab

1. With nothing in the chart selected, click on one of the bars. This will select all of the bars.

2. Then click on the one bar you want to select for the color change, in this case the "Average for M-7" bar. This selects just that bar.

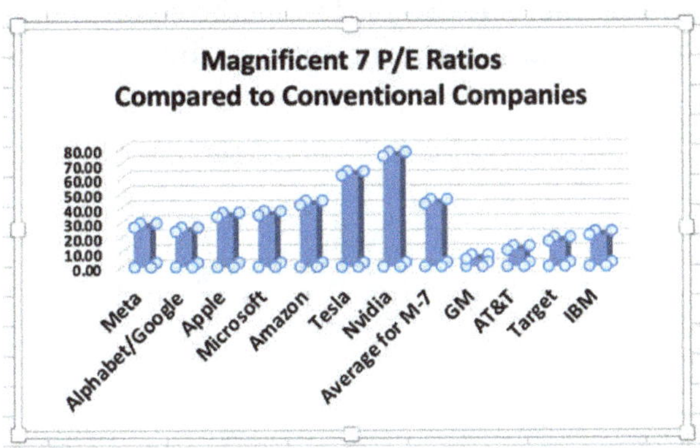

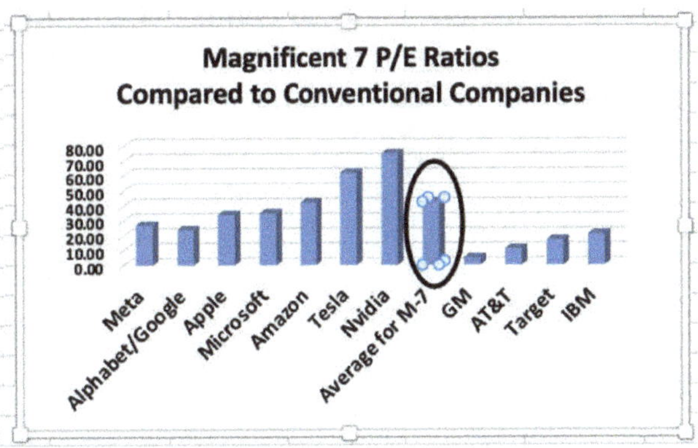

3. Click the Format tab on the Excel menu bar (look to the far right).

On the right side, there should be a panel that opens with a tab for the paint bucket tool. If you don't see the panel, here's how to find it.

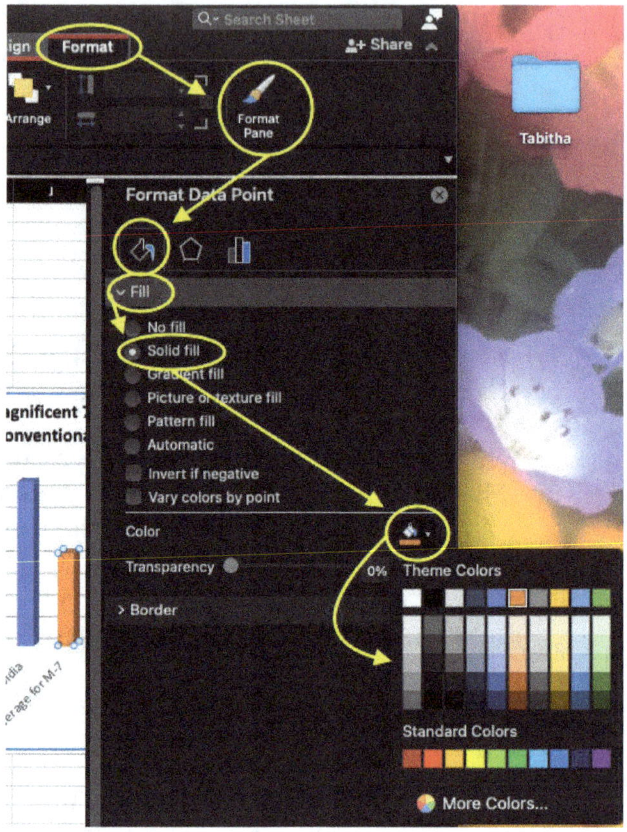

4. In for Format section, click the Format Pane symbol (Paintbrush) to display the Format pane.

5. In the Format pane, click the paint bucket tab.

6. Then click the > symbol next to the word "Fill" to expand the Fill options. If the arrow is pointing down, the Fill options are already expanded.

7. Select Solid fill, and then in the same section of the pane, find the word "Color" and click the paint bucket button to open a color picker window.

8. Select the color. This will close the color picker window.

9. Close the format pane by clicking the round X button on the pane's upper right.

There is an easier way to change the colors of the bar. But the pathway above offers far more formatting options. For a simpler way to change the color of a bar, use the following short-cut instructions.

Formatting Bars Via Home Tab

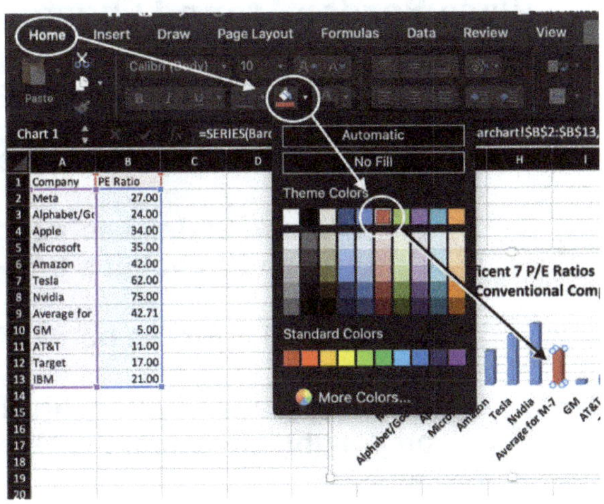

1. **Select the bar you want to color.**
2. **Click on the Home tab in the Excel menu.**
3. **In the Font section of the ribbon, click the Paint Bucket color-fill symbol.**
4. **Select a color from the color picker pop-up.**

Note: It's the same process you used to color-fill a cell or header as shown in previous lessons.

5. **To color the last 4 bars red, select the GM bar and use either method to color it, then select the next bar and repeat.**

When you are done, your chart should look like the one below, minus the border.

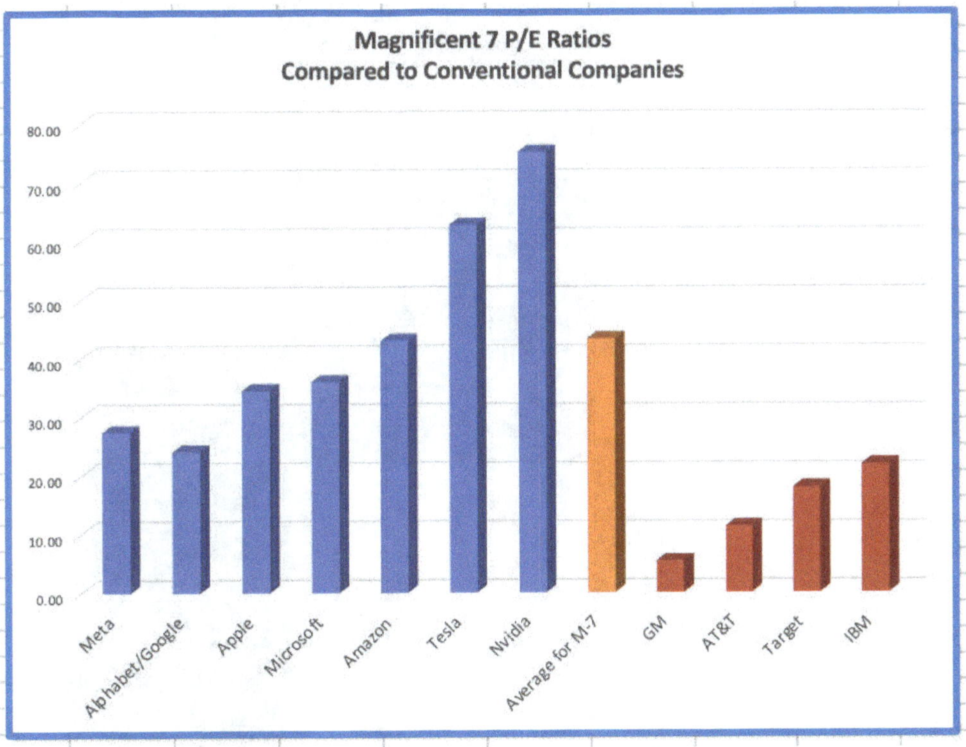

Place Border Around Chart:

1. **Make sure your chart is selected.**
2. **Click on the Format tab in the Excel menu.**
3. **In the Shape Styles section of the ribbon, click the down-arrow next to the blue crayon symbol (it's tiny, see below).**
4. **Select a color for the border from the color picker pop-up.**
5. **Click the crayon symbol again, and from the color picker, hover your pointer on <u>Weight</u> and select the "Weight" or thickness of the border.**

Go ahead and play around with the colors and the thickness to get a feel for this tool.

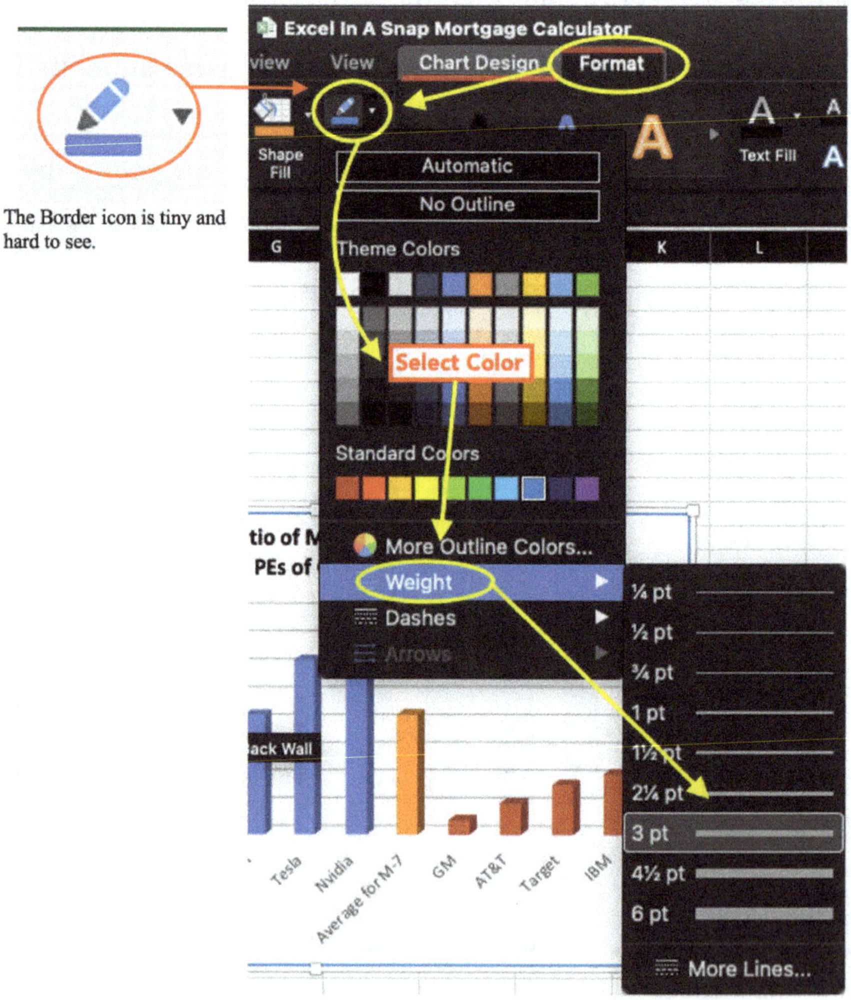

The Border icon is tiny and hard to see.

Line Chart

To create a line chart, you should have at least a dozen data points. We are going to create a graph that charts the quarterly sales totals for an imaginary company. We will start with Q1 of 2020 and end with Q4 of 2023.

To get started, move on to tab <u>6. Line Chart</u> in the Excel workbook downloaded from INaSnapGuides.com, or:

1. **Open a new sheet by pressing the + symbol at the bottom of the window to the right of the worksheet tabs, and fill it out as you see in this screenshot.**
    a. **Cell A1:**

       Quarter

    b. **Cell A2:**

       Q1 2020

    c. **Cell A3:**

       Q2 2020

    d. **Cell A4:**

       Q3 2020

    e. **Cell A5:**

       Q4 2020

    f. **Cell B1:**

       Sales Totals in 1,000s

	A	B
1	Quarter	Sales Totals in 1,000s
2	Q1 2020	
3	Q2 2020	
4	Q3 2020	
5	Q4 2020	

	A	B
1	**Quarter**	**Sales Totals in 1,000s**
2	Q1 2020	527
3	Q2 2020	466
4	Q3 2020	401
5	Q4 2020	378
6	Q1 2021	385
7	Q2 2021	421
8	Q3 2021	553
9	Q4 2021	456
10	Q1 2022	276
11	Q2 2022	456
12	Q3 2022	789
13	Q4 2022	345
14	Q1 2023	678
15	Q2 2023	345
16	Q3 2023	567
17	Q4 2023	345

2. **Select A2-A5 and copy it down to A-17.**

Reminder: Select the cells, hover over them until you see the black plus sign in the corner, then click and drag it down to cell A-17.

Once all of the quarters are filled in, fill out Column B as shown above. If you want to save time, you can just type in your own made-up numbers and it would be a good idea to stick to 3 digits.

3. **With the entire table selected (as shown on prior page) click the <u>Insert</u> tab in the Excel menu.**

4. **In the Charts section of the ribbon, click the down-arrow next to the line chart symbol, which displays a pop-up window with all the line graph styles Excel offers.**

5. **Select the first graph in the top row of the line graph styles.**

This will both create a line graph using the data you selected, AND display the Chart Design ribbon. As long as the chart is selected, the Chart Design tab will be available.

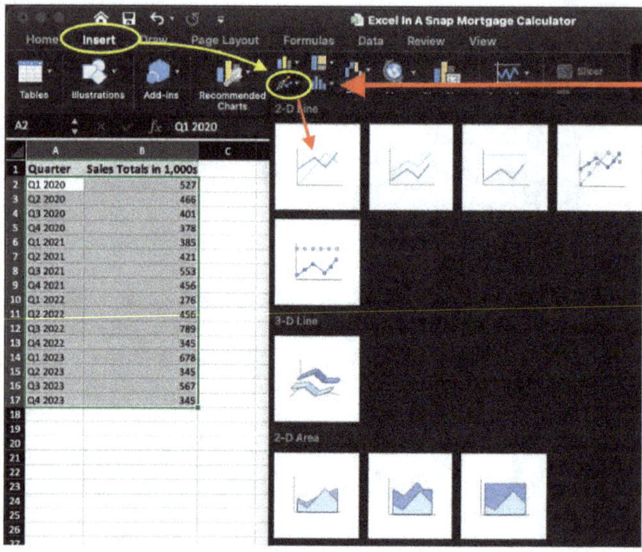

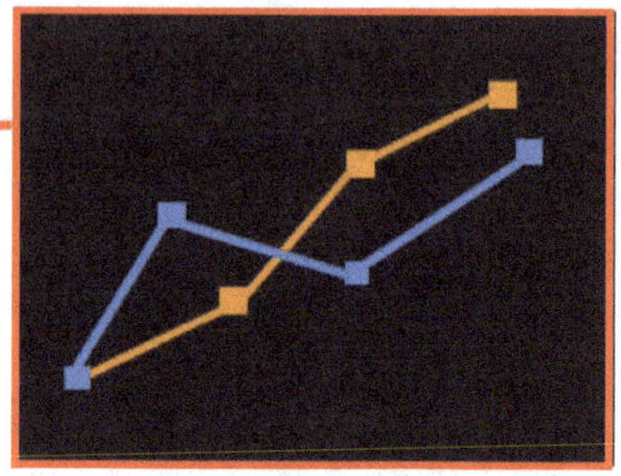

The Line Graph icon is also very small and hard to see.

6. **If you accidently click elsewhere in the app window that causes the Chart Design tab to disappear, simply click on the chart again to make the tab reappear.**

I've found it easiest to select the first graph, and then use the *Chart Design* tab to select the style of chart you would like from the ribbon. See below.

Once you've opened the Chart Designs (above) play around to get acquainted with this feature. Use the < and > buttons at either end of the Chart Styles ribbon to see more options.

Pie Chart

Inserting Data From A Different Worksheet

In the workbook downloaded from INaSnapGuides.com, select sheet tab 6. Pie Chart. Or create a new worksheet using the + symbol at the bottom of the window next to the worksheet tabs, and name it Pie Chart.

Pie charts are fairly straightforward and are useful for showing how a specific resource is distributed across several categories. In this lesson, we're going to construct one for a household budget. Remember when I told you we would need the Mortgage Calculator we created for our pie chart project?

We'll take the monthly mortgage P&I payment from the table and input it into a pie chart. This way, whenever we update the total mortgage amount, our pie chart budget will automatically update, even if it's on a different worksheet!

The click-path is surprisingly simple.

1. **If you don't have the downloaded workbook, fill out your spreadsheet as shown below.**

2. **Merge Cells A1 and B1 to create the worksheet's header.**

	A	B
1	Monthly Household Budget	
2	Groceries	$300.00
3	Utilities	$215.00
4	Transportation	$166.00
5	Entertainment	$200.00
6	Mortgage Payment	

We haven't filled in cell B6 yet because we need to be prepared to execute this task.

First of all, locate the Mortgage Calculator sheet. If you need to move the Pie Chart sheet tab closer to the Mortgage Calculator sheet tab, you can do this by clicking and dragging the tab.

3. Read this before proceeding. In cell B6, type an = sign. Then, click the Mortgage Calculator sheet tab at the bottom of the screen, then click on cell B9.

   Once you have typed in the equal sign (=) in cell B6, do not click anywhere *except* the Mortgage Calculator sheet tab. If you do click out of the cell and then click back in, this action won't work. If you make that mistake, just delete the equal sign, exit the cell, select it again, type in = once more, and proceed with the next steps. While these steps are simple and few, you must execute them exactly in order or it won't work.

4. Select cell B6 in the Pie Chart worksheet and type in = as shown below on the left.

5. Click on the sheet tab for Mortgage Calculator.

6. Click cell B9 and hit Return/Enter.

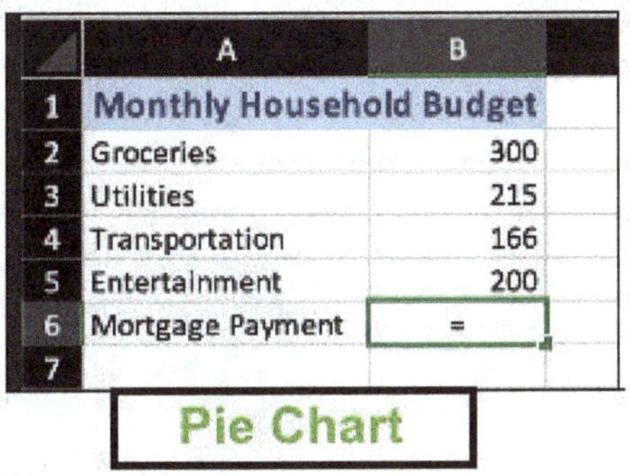

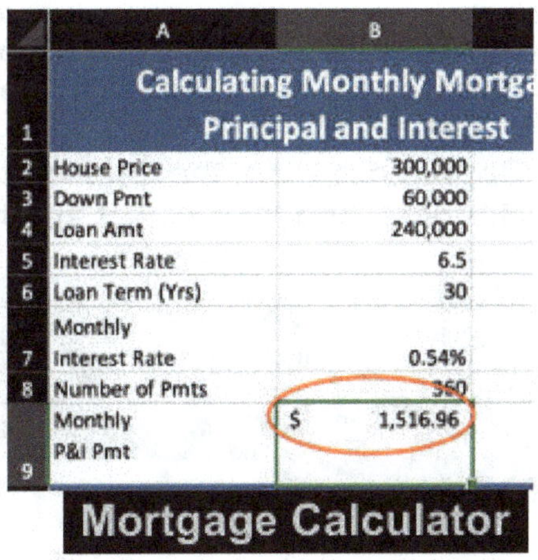

Once you hit Return/Enter, Excel instantly returns to cell B6 on the Pie Chart worksheet which is now filled with the mortgage payment amount from Cell B9 in the Mortgage Calculator worksheet, which should be 1,516.96.

Notice the formula in the Formula Bar for B6 in the Pie Chart worksheet contains the reference for cell B9 of the <u>Mortgage Calculator</u> sheet; i.e., *='Mortgage CalculatorCalculate Mo'!B9*. Recall that you entered a mortgage payment formula in cell B9 in the Mortgage Calculator table. The *'Calculate Mo'* part of the reference refers to that mortgage formula. The ! symbol in the formula indicates that the text preceding it is a reference from a different worksheet in the same workbook.

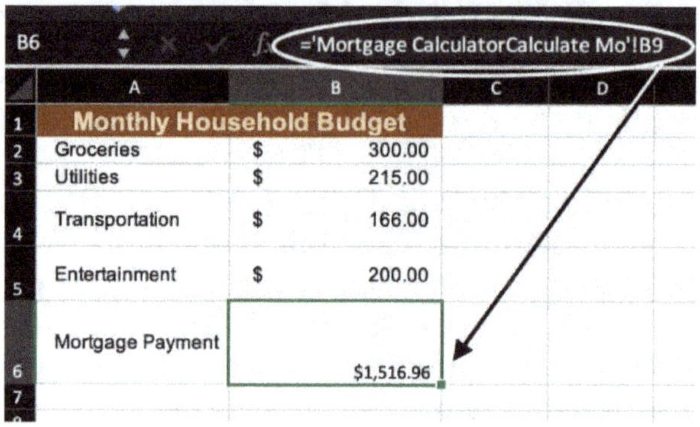

7. **Select cells B2 through B6 and then convert the numbers to dollar amounts (Home tab in the Excel menu > Number section > Number Format drop down).**

Now let's construct our pie chart.

8. **Select cells A2 through B6.**

9. **Click the Insert tab in the Excel menu, and then the pie chart symbol in the Chart section of the ribbon, select the 3-D pie chart.**

10. **Double-click on the title of the pie chart and type "Monthly Household Budget," and then select anything outside of the chart title text box.**

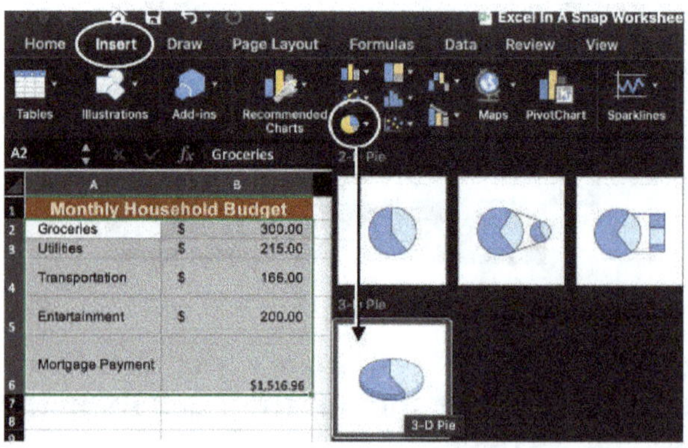

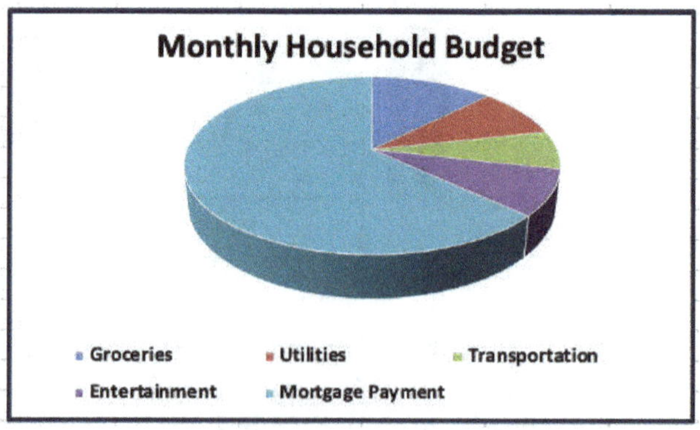

Let's play around with this.

11. Go to the Mortgage Calculator worksheet and change the house price (in cell B2) from $300,000 to $200,000. Hit Return/Enter.

Return to the Pie Chart worksheet containing the Household Budget to see the difference in both the Mortgage Payment value in cell B6, and the make-up of the pie chart.

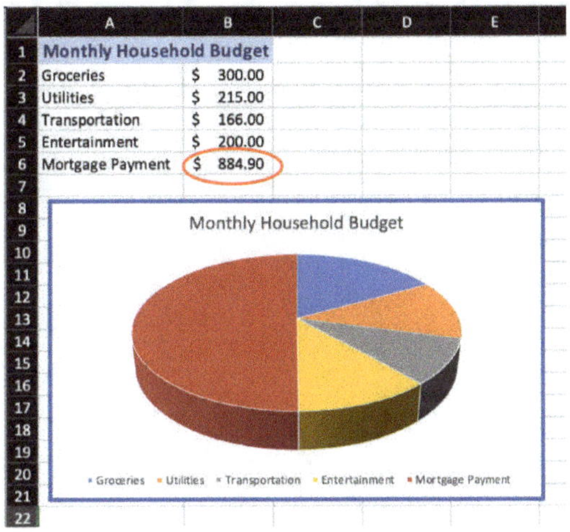

Congratulations on completing the basics of "Excel In A Snap." With this newfound expertise, you can now tackle most Excel-related tasks with confidence.

However, many professions, especially those in sales and marketing, require the use of Excel's advanced features, such as Pivot Tables and VLookup.

These powerful tools will enable you to compile and analyze valuable information from various data sources, making it easier to evaluate sales, marketing, and budgeting data, as well as perform complex sorting and filtering tasks.

Don't worry if the upcoming section demands a bit more of your time. The advanced skills you're about to acquire will elevate you to an elite level of Excel proficiency, a status achieved by only a select few.

BONUS SECTION
Pivot Tables & VLookup

PROJECT 7: Pivot Tables

Pivot tables provide advanced sorting and filtering features for large, complex data sets. With Pivot Tables, you can determine how much revenue a business generates from individual products or services. Or which months have the highest sales. You can get an incredible amount of data from the various sorting and filtering actions made possible by Pivot Tables.

On the downloaded *Excel In A Snap Project Worksheets* file, you can find the data table shown below on the worksheet tab: 7. Pivot Table Data Set.

If you prefer to fill out the data on your own, create a new worksheet and name it Pivot Table Data Set.

Here is the data table below. This data tracks events and revenues for a concert hall.

Note: This table has 25 entries and continues on to the next page.

	A	B	C	D	E	F
1	Date	Event Name	Performer	Genre	Tickets Sold	Revenue
2	01/10/2024	Jazz Night	The Jazz Cats	Jazz	120	2400
3	01/12/2024	Soul Session	Smooth Vibes	Soul	130	2600
4	01/15/2024	Rock Fest	Rock Legends	Rock	300	7500
5	01/17/2024	Pop Stars Live	The Pop Wonders	Pop	220	6600
6	01/20/2024	Classical Eve	Symphony Stars	Classical	200	5000
7	01/22/2024	Hip-Hop Hits	Rhyme Masters	Hip-Hop	180	3600
8	01/25/2024	Blues Bash	Blue Notes	Blues	150	3000
9	01/28/2024	Indie Night	Indie Vibes	Indie	180	3600
10	02/01/2024	Reggae Rhythms	Island Vibes	Reggae	170	3400
11	02/05/2024	Country Fair	Country Roads	Country	220	4400
1	02/07/202	Latin Fiesta	Salsa	Latin	190	3800

2	4		Sensation			
13	02/10/2024	Funky Groove	The Funk Squad	Funk	160	3200
14	02/13/2024	Jazz Legends	Sax Masters	Jazz	210	4200
15	02/15/2024	Rock Revival	Electric Dreams	Rock	250	6250
16	02/18/2024	Classical Morning	Morning Strings	Classical	170	4250
17	02/20/2024	Pop Celebration	Urban Pop	Pop	260	7800
18	02/22/2024	Soulful Evening	Deep Soul	Soul	140	2800
19	02/25/2024	Blues & Brews	Midnight Blues	Blues	160	3200
20	02/28/2024	Indie Jam	The Indie Wave	Indie	200	4000
21	03/02/2024	Hip-Hop Classics	Beat Busters	Hip-Hop	190	3800
22	03/05/2024	Latin Nights	Tropical Beats	Latin	180	3600
23	03/08/2024	Funk Fest	Groove Masters	Funk	210	4200
24	03/10/2024	Reggae Sunset	Island Stars	Reggae	200	4000
25	03/12/2024	Country Legends	The Country Kings	Country	230	4600

1. On the Excel menu, click the Insert tab, and then, in the Tables section of the ribbon, click Pivot Table.

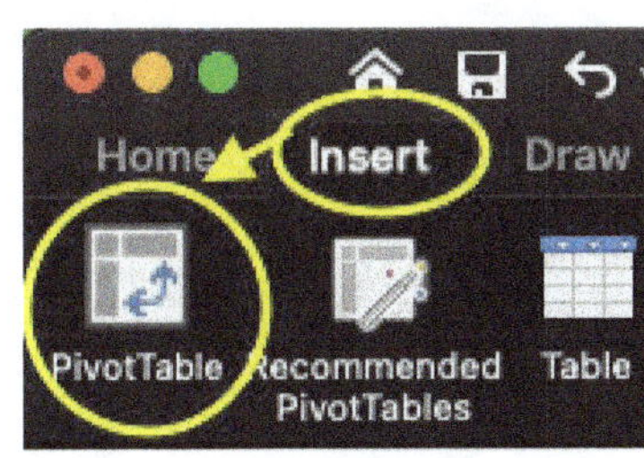

2. In the pop-up that opens, make sure New Worksheet is selected and click OK. (screenshot below)

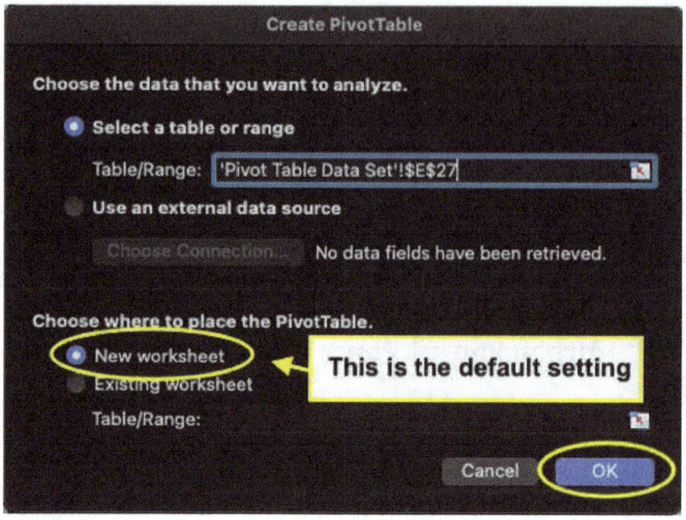
Create PivotTable
Choose the data that you want to analyze.
Select a table or range
Table/Range:
'Pivot Table Data Set'!$E$27
Use an external data source
Choose Connection...
No data fields have been retrieved.
Choose where to place the PivotTable.
New worksheet
Existing worksheet
Table/Range:
This is the default setting
Cancel
OK

This will automatically take you to a new sheet. The new sheet tab will appear to the immediate left of your datasheet tab.

3. **Double-click on the tab of the new sheet (at the bottom of the Excel window) and name it 'Pivot Table Concert Hall'.**

The two sheet tabs should look like the image below.

Add Pivot Table To Same Sheet As Dataset

If you want your Pivot Table to stay on the same page as your data table, you must input the coordinates of where you would like the upper left-hand corner of the Pivot Table to land.

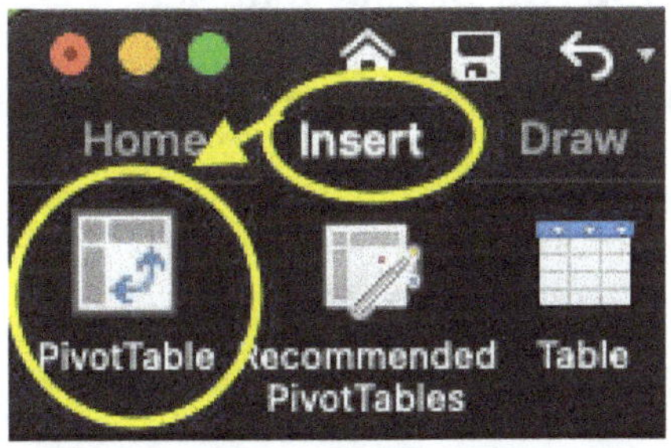

Once your data is set up, create the Pivot Table:

1. **Select the entire data set, including the header row.**
2. **On the taskbar, click <u>InsertàPivot Table</u>.**
3. **In the pop-up select <u>Existing worksheet</u>.**
4. **In the Table/Range slot input H2; or you can click on cell H2 to automatically enter it.**
5. **Click <u>OK.</u>**

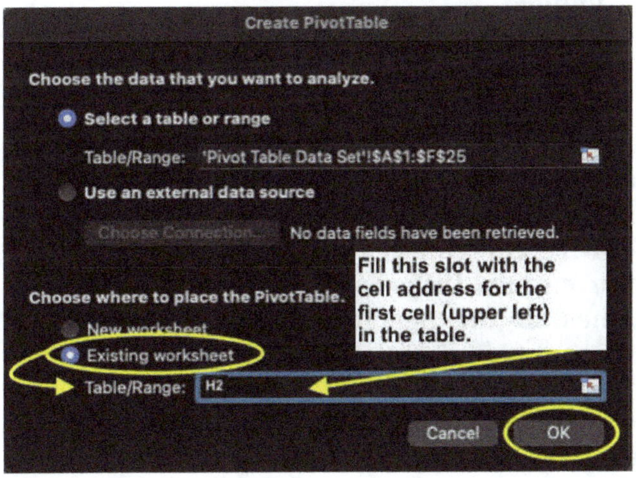

Pivot Table Fields

A Pivot Table will appear to the right of your table. If you can't see it, drag the right edge of the Excel window to the right.

Click on the Pivot Table to open the <u>PivotTable Fields</u> panel. If you click anywhere outside the pivot table, the Pivot Table panel will disappear. Simply click back in the pivot table again to make the pane reappear. This is the work bench.

The <u>Field Name</u> section at the top of the pane displays a list of the column headers in the top row of your data set.

Below the field names are four sectors:

1. **Filters**
2. **Columns**
3. **Rows**
4. **Values**

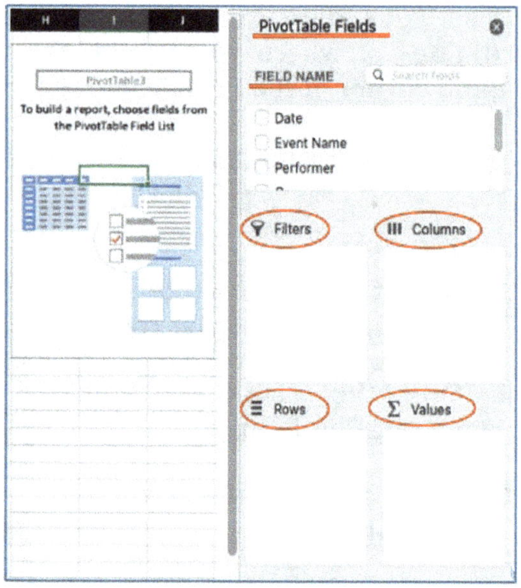

When you drag-and-drop a Field Name into one of the four sectors, the Pivot Table will organize that information into a table, allowing the viewer to quickly obtain vital information. Different variations of Field Names in the Sector boxes will provide different types of information.

Let's take this Pivot Table out on the road. First, we will examine ticket sales and revenues by venue.

Creating Your First Pivot Table

1. **Drag-and-drop <u>Event Name</u> into the <u>Rows</u> sector.**

   The Pivot Table will change to reflect your data choice as shown below on the right.

2. **Drag and drop <u>Performer</u> into the <u>Rows</u> sector.**

   Now the Pivot Table shows you all the upcoming events matched with the performers booked for the event.

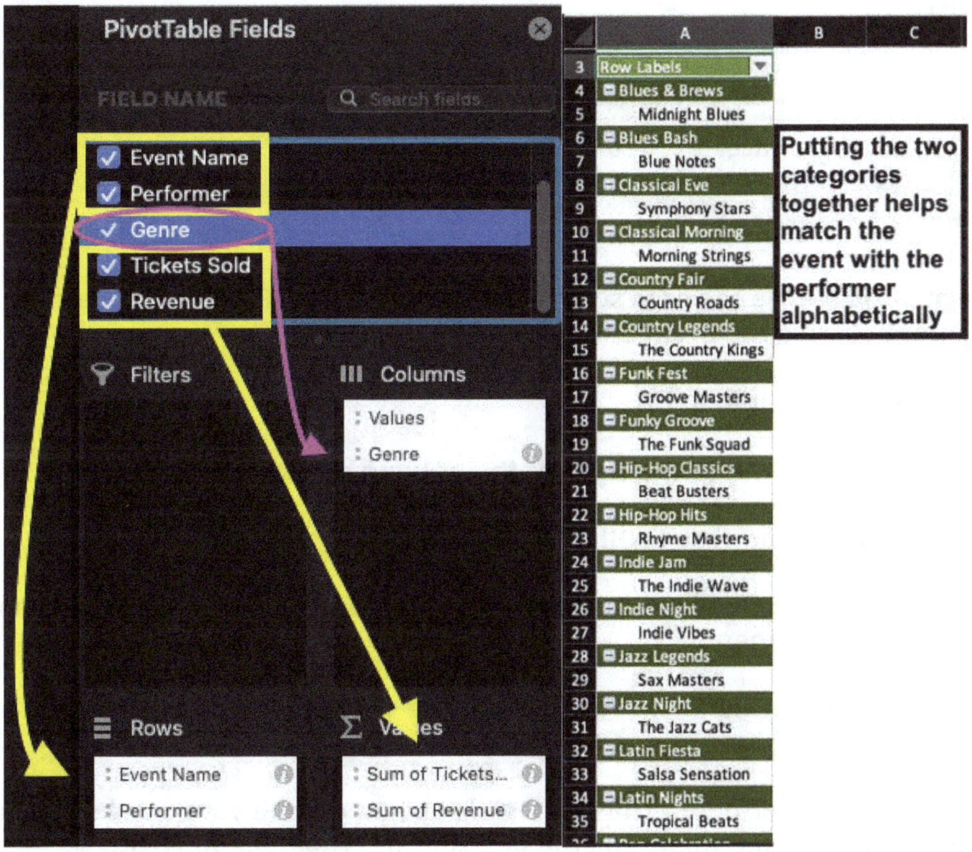

If you accidentally dragged the field name to the wrong sector, click and drag it out of the pane to remove it, or drag it to the sector where you want it to appear. You may need to click back into the pane to make it update.

3. **Drag-and-drop <u>Tickets Sold</u> and <u>Revenue</u> into the <u>Values</u> sector.**

4. **Drag-and-drop <u>Genre</u> into the <u>Column</u> sector.**

Notice that “Values” is also shown in the Columns sector.

As you can see in the image below, both the "Genres" (Blues, Classical, etc.) and the "Values" (sum of "Tickets Sold" and "Revenue") are listed horizontally on the Pivot Table spreadsheet as column headings.

Now the Pivot Table is spread out wide. But it provides important data. The booking agent for the concert hall can easily see which groups and which genres are generating the most revenue and which are generating the least.

	Column Labels				
	Blues		Classical		Country
Row Labels	Sum of Tickets Sold	Sum of Revenue (in $)	Sum of Tickets Sold	Sum of Revenue (in $)	Sum of Ticl
Blues & Brews	**160**	**3200**			
Midnight Blues	160	3200			
Blues Bash	**150**	**3000**			
Blue Notes	150	3000			
Classical Eve			**200**	**5000**	
Symphony Stars			200	5000	
Classical Morning			**170**	**4250**	
Morning Strings			170	4250	
Country Fair					

With this data configuration managers can see which venues sell the most tickets and create the most revenue.

This information will be easier to scan if you use the Freeze Panes tool to lock the "Row Labels" column listing the Event and Performer categories.

Freeze Panes Reminder:

1. **Select the column to the right of the column you want to freeze.**

(I want to freeze Column-H so I will select Column-I)

2. **For PC: On the Excel menu, click the View tab to open the pop-up, and then click Freeze Panes.**

3. **For Mac: From the Menu App bar on the very top of your computer screen, click Window, then Freeze Panes.**

Now hover your pointer below the last visible row of cells in your worksheet to make the scroll bar appear, and then slide the horizontal scroll left and right.

Tip: If you Freeze Panes and notice that several columns on the left disappear, just Unfreeze Panes to get them back.

Sort by Date on Pivot Tables

Most companies like to see how much money they are bringing in on certain dates. They may want to know if they are making more money on certain weekdays than on others. Or if some months bring in more business than others. This is one more way Pivot Tables can track sales.

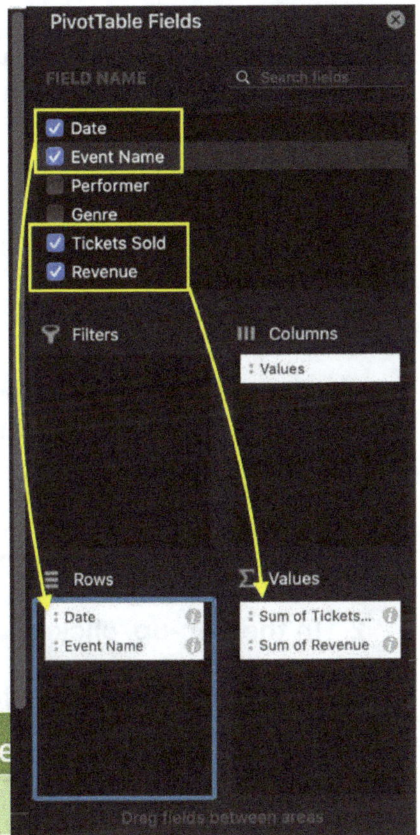

1. **Clear all of the filters by dragging the names back to the <u>Field Name</u> area above. Or, find the categories in the Field Name box, and then un-tick the check boxes.**

2. **Drag the <u>Date</u> and <u>Event Name</u> fields down to the <u>Rows</u> section (see screenshot).**

3. **Drag the <u>Tickets Sold</u> and <u>Revenue</u> fields down to the Values section.**

Make sure the category names appear in the order shown in the screenshot. If any are out of order, simply drag the category name to the desired place.

The resulting Pivot Table should look like the one below. The top row that shows <1/10/24 doesn't apply in this case since none of the dates precede that one, so we can ignore it.

Row Labels	Sum of Tickets Sold	Sum of Reve
⊞ <1/10/24		
⊞ Jan	1480	34300
⊞ Feb	2130	47300
⊞ Mar	1010	20200
Grand Total	4620	101800

This Pivot Table shows us the total tickets sold and the total revenues for each month.

If you would like to view the total tickets sold and revenues by each day, click the plus sign next to the month on the left to expand the list.

If you don't see a plus sign next to the months, move on to the following instructions.

Row Labels	Sum of Tickets Sold	Sum of Revenue
⊞ <1/10/24		
⊟ Jan	1480	34300
⊟ 10-Jan	120	2400
Jazz Night	120	2400
⊟ 12-Jan	130	2600
Soul Session	130	2600
⊟ 15-Jan	300	7500
Rock Fest	300	7500
⊟ 17-Jan	220	6600
Pop Stars Live	220	6600
⊟ 20-Jan	200	5000
Classical Eve	200	5000
⊟ 22-Jan	180	3600
Hip-Hop Hits	180	3600
⊟ 25-Jan	150	3000
Blues Bash	150	3000
⊟ 28-Jan	180	3600
Indie Night	180	3600
⊞ Feb	2130	47300
⊞ Mar	1010	20200
Grand Total	4620	101800

If the Pivot table only shows the months, or just the days, here is how you can fine-tune the dates.

1. **Select any of the months (or dates) and then right-click on the cell.**
2. **In the pop-up, click on Group.**
3. **In the next pop-up, click-and-hold on Days, and then drag down to select both Days and Months. Or, you can click on Days, press the Shift key on your keyboard, and then click on Months. Click OK.**

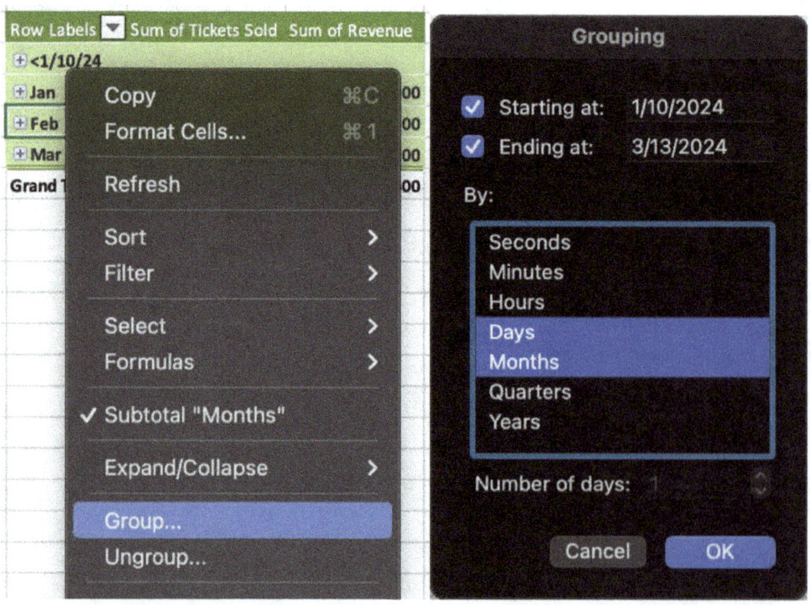

This will create the same type of table as shown in the screenshot below, a monthly list that can expand to show the days.

Row Labels	Sum of Tickets Sold	Sum of Revenue
⊞<1/10/24		
⊟Jan	1480	34300
⊟10-Jan	120	2400
Jazz Night	120	2400
⊟12-Jan	130	2600
Soul Session	130	2600
⊟15-Jan	300	7500
Rock Fest	300	7500
⊟17-Jan	220	6600
Pop Stars Live	220	6600
⊟20-Jan	200	5000
Classical Eve	200	5000
⊟22-Jan	180	3600
Hip-Hop Hits	180	3600
⊟25-Jan	150	3000
Blues Bash	150	3000
⊟28-Jan	180	3600
Indie Night	180	3600
⊞Feb	2130	47300
⊞Mar	1010	20200
Grand Total	4620	101800

Filter Option For Genre

Now let's see how ticket sales and revenues perform just by genre. See if you can figure out how to do this on your own before following the instructions below. Before you begin, clear the categories from the four sectors to start with a clean slate.

1. **Drag the Genre category into the Rows sector.**
2. **Drag the Tickets Sold and the Revenues categories into the Values sector.**
3. **You should wind up with a table similar to the one on the right.**

Row Labels	Sum of Tickets Sold	Sum of Revenue (in $)
Blues	310	6200
Classical	370	9250
Country	450	9000
Funk	370	7400
Hip-Hop	370	7400
Indie	380	7600
Jazz	330	6600
Latin	370	7400
Pop	480	14400
Reggae	370	7400
Rock	550	13750
Soul	270	5400
Grand Total	4620	101800

Sort By Month On Pivot Tables

If you are experiencing some déjà vu it's because we just did this. But sorting by month is complicated enough, we need to do it again to get the hang of it. This time we'll do it somewhat differently by placing the revenues in descending order so the highest-earning months are on top.

1. **Clear the four sectors.**

2. **Drag the Date Field to the Rows sector.**

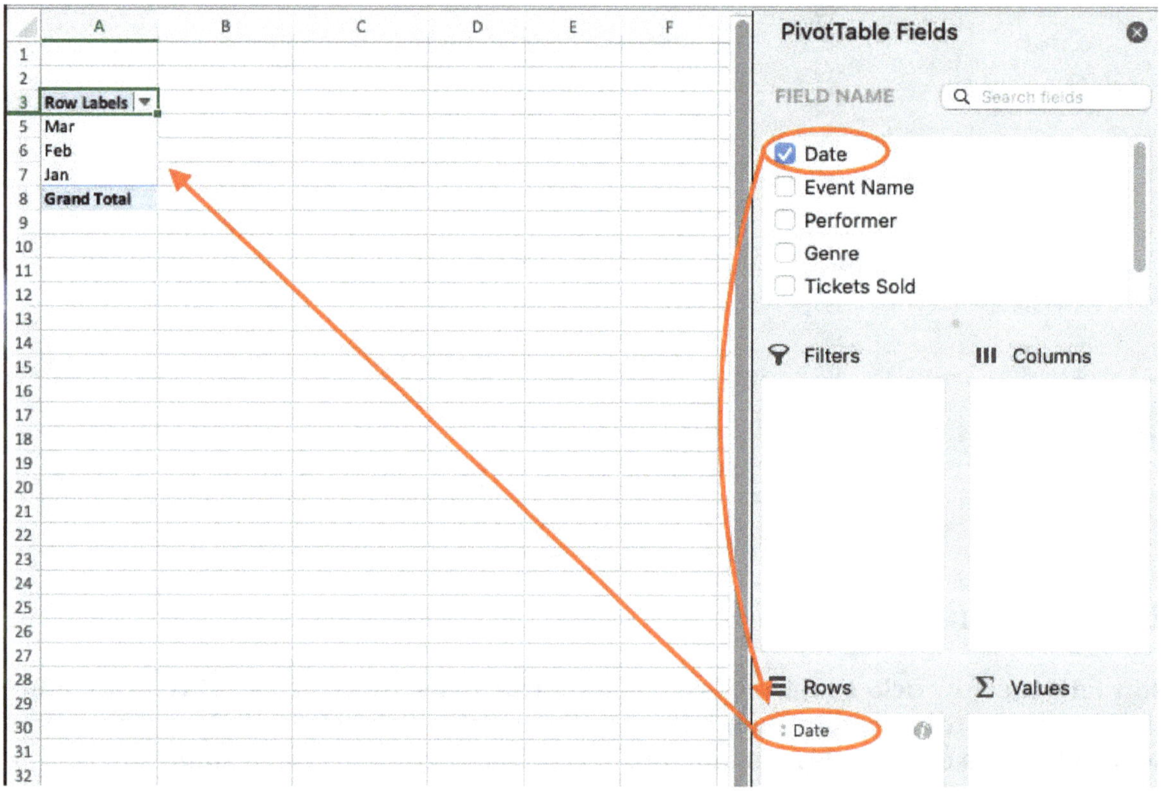

3. Right-click on any month in the Pivot Table.

4. From the popup menu, choose <u>Group</u>.

5. In the next pop-up select <u>Months</u> and click <u>OK.</u>

6. Drag the <u>Tickets Sold</u> field and the <u>Revenue</u> field into the <u>Values</u> sector.

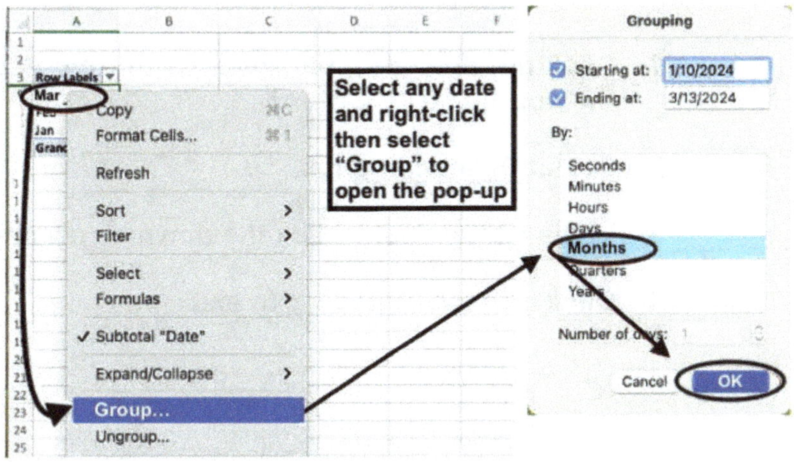

The Columns sector will automatically be filled with the heading <u>Values</u>. This signals that the <u>Sum of Revenues</u> and <u>Sum of Tickets Sold</u> will be featured in columns on your Pivot Table. This allows the viewer to see how much revenue is being generated month by month.

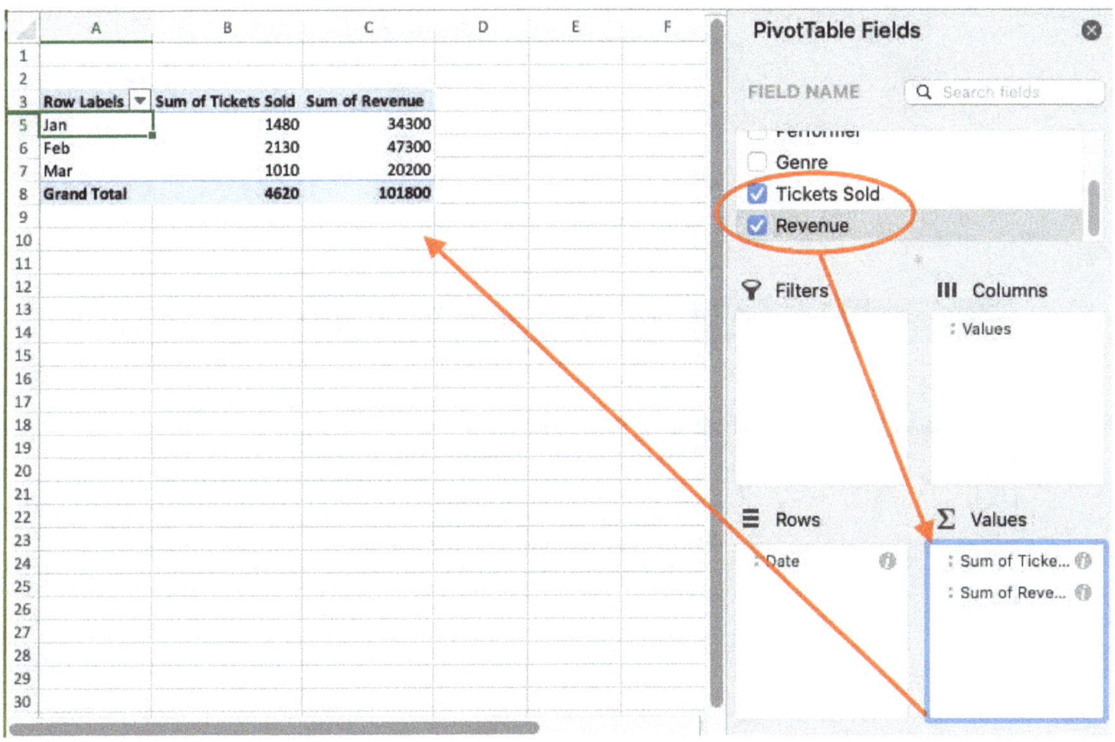

Now we will sort to find the most profitable months.

1. Click the drop-down arrow next to Row Labels in your Pivot Table to open the pop-up.
2. Select Descending tab.
3. In the Sort by field, click the down-arrow and select Sum of Revenue.
4. Click outside of pop-up to exit.

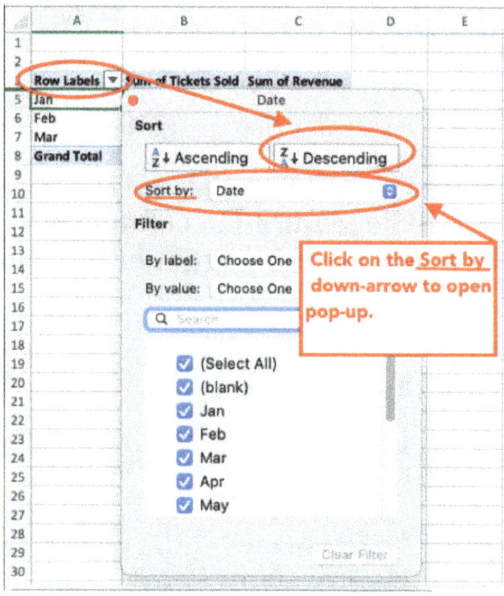

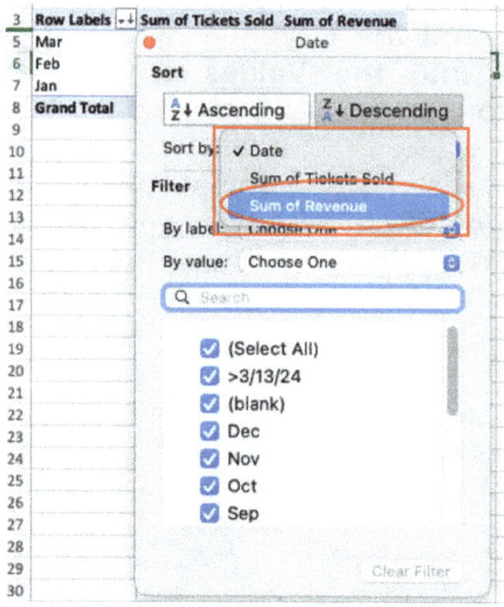

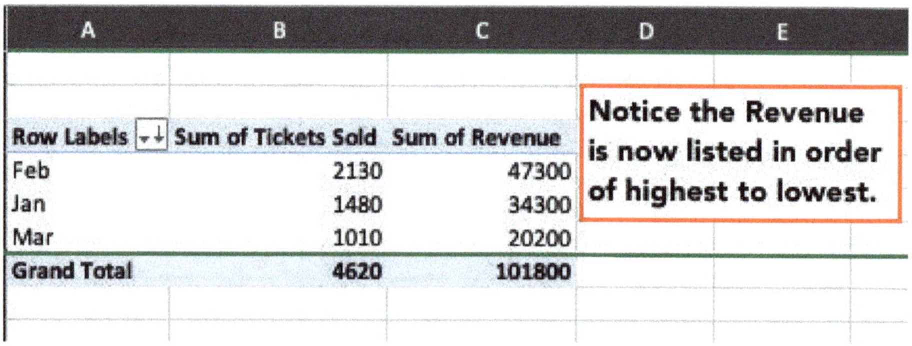

Row Labels	Sum of Tickets Sold	Sum of Revenue
Feb	2130	47300
Jan	1480	34300
Mar	1010	20200
Grand Total	4620	101800

Collapsible Lists

This concert hall pivot table provides an ideal opportunity to apply the collapsible list tool. So, before we finish up, let's learn this useful function.

1. **Go to the Concert Hall Table (the original data set) and select all of the rows for January (Rows 2—9).**

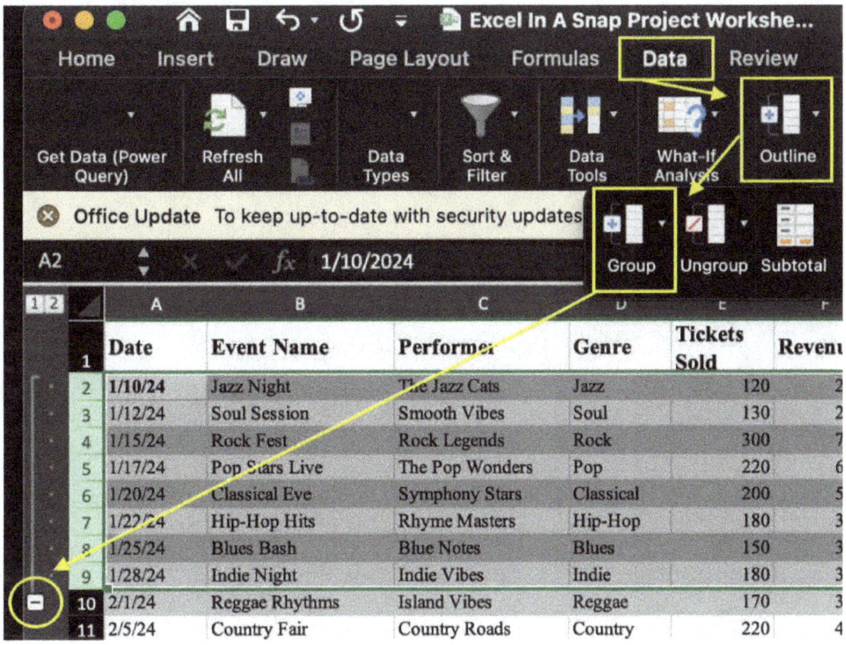

2. **On the Excel menu bar, click the <u>Data</u> tab.**

3. **Click the down arrow on the <u>Outline</u> symbol.**

4. **Click the <u>Group</u> icon.**

(You don't have to click the down arrow).

5. **In the popup, select <u>Rows</u> and click OK.**

Notice the thin gray vertical line that appears just to the left of the row numbers.

6. **To collapse the rows, go to the thin gray vertical line on the left and click the tiny white box with the minus sign at the bottom of the line. When you do, the rows will disappear along with the gray line. In its place, you'll find a tiny white box with a plus sign.**

7. **Click the "+" box to expand the rows.**

8. **Now, to Ungroup the rows, select them (while they're expanded) and use the same actions in step 2, but this time, click <u>Ungroup</u>.**

9. **Tip: If you accidently ungroup them while they are collapsed, you can double-click on the horizontal green line between row numbers 1 and 10 to get the hidden rows back.**

Congratulations! You have now learned Pivot Tables, one of the advanced features of Excel that's often overlooked by many users. Well done! Let's continue with the final project in this book; VLookup.

PROJECT 8: VLookup

VLookup allows you to look up specific information on a table of data. A simple menu with different sizes and prices for items is ideal to show how VLookup works. You can either use the table provided in the downloaded *Excel In A Snap Project Worksheets* file, or you can construct your own on a new sheet.

1. **From the downloaded file, select Worksheet tab: 8. VLookup Menu. Otherwise, set up the first VLookup table as follows.**

	A	B	C	D
1	**Pastry**	**Single**	**Half Dozen**	**Full Dozen**
2	Glazed Donuts	$ 1.50	$ 7.50	$ 15.00
3	Buttermilk Donuts	$ 1.75	$ 9.00	$ 18.00
4	Jelly Donuts	$ 2.00	$ 10.50	$ 21.00
5	Bear Claws	$ 2.50	$ 13.50	$ 27.00
6	Cherry Tarts	$ 3.50	$ 19.50	$ 39.00
7	Macaroons	$ 2.50	$ 13.50	$ 27.00
8	Chocolate Eclairs	$ 3.00	$ 16.50	$ 33.00
9	Wedding cookies	$ 1.00	$ 6.00	$ 12.00
10				
11	Question: What is the price of a half dozen Macaroons?			
12				
13	Macaroons			

2. **Type in just the numbers. Then select them all and add the dollar formatting.**

   a. **With <u>Home</u> tab selected, look for $ sign symbol or % symbol on taskbar.**

   b. **Click the down arrow, select "<u>$ English (United States)</u>."**

Before we conjure up the VLookup tool, we need to be clear on what we're looking for. We will start by writing out our questions. This will help us focus on our end goal as we go through the complicated process of setting up our VLookup formula.

1. **Click into cell A11 and write "Question: What is the price of a half dozen Macaroons?"**

2. **Now click on cell A13 and write "Macaroons" (make sure you get the spelling right).**

Let's break down the VLookup formula to understand its core function before starting our projects.

VLOOKUP(lookup_value,table_array,col_index_num,[range_lookup])

The part of the formula within the parentheses are the *parameters* **for the formula, and the data that goes into each parameter is an** *argument.*

If you are familiar with the Pythagorean theorem, you'll remember that $a^2 + b^2 = c^2$**. In this formula,** *a*, *b*, **and** *c* **represent the height, length, and hypotenuse; these are the** *parameters***. But the value of each of the parameters, like a=1; and b=2; is an** *argument***. When you change an argument in a formula, the output changes with it. For instance, if you change the argument to a=3 and b=5, the output of the formula would change.**

When you are inputting this formula, keep in mind the values for each argument are separated by a comma and there are no spaces.

Tip: The data you are searching for must be in a column to the right of the lookup value.

> **lookup_value:** **The lookup_value argument is directly related to the thing you are looking for. In this case we are looking for the price of a macaroon, so the macaroon is the lookup_value. The price of the macaroon will be found in the table_array.**

table_array: The table-array argument is a range of all the cells you will be searching through, in this case all the different pastries and the prices which are located in the range of cells A2 through D9.

col_index_num: This argument is the number of the column that contains the data you are looking for. We will be looking in the column of the half-dozen count or Column C which, in this case, is column 3. You type in only the number 3.

[range_lookup]: This argument reflects our decision to look for an approximate match, or an exact match by choosing either TRUE or FALSE. As soon as you add a comma after the column number, a popup appears offering the TRUE/FALSE options with explanations for each.

When choosing between an approximate match or an exact match, you must ignore the literal meaning of TRUE and FALSE. In this case, the two words are just codes. Select 'TRUE' when looking for an approximate match and 'FALSE' when looking for an exact match. It doesn't make sense, so don't think about it too much.

Notice that [range_lookup] is surrounded by square brackets. In Excel, this usually means the parameter is optional, and if left out, the formula will use the default value for the argument. For VLookup, the default argument for [range_lookup] is TRUE. Let's do this!

1. **Put your pointer in cell B13 and type =VLOOKUP.**

Before you're done typing, a pop-up will appear. Select VLOOKUP.

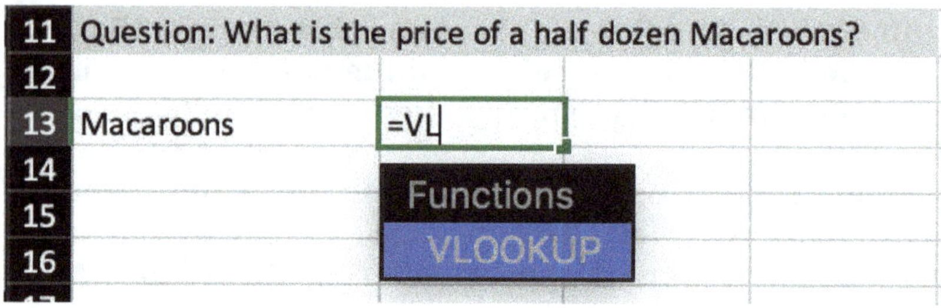

Once you select VLOOKUP, the formula popup will appear as shown below.

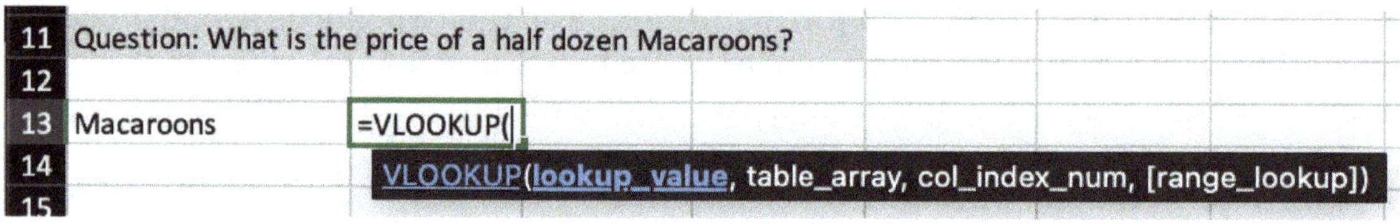

2. **To enter lookup_value, click on "Macaroon" in cell A13.**
   a. **When A13 appears in the formula, type a comma. This will take you to the next argument.**
3. **To input table_array:**
   a. **Select Cells A2 through D9.**
   b. **When 'A2:D9' appears in the formula, type a comma to go to the next argument.**
4. **To input col_index_num (the column number):**
   a. **Type 3 followed by a comma to go to the next argument.**

Reminder: The numeral 3 in the *col_index_num* argument represents the third column in the menu table, and NOT the third column of the worksheet.

This distinction is very important. In this lesson, the third column of the table coincidentally occupies the third column of the worksheet, but don't let that confuse you.

We want the data in the third column of the Menu table, the column that contains the various prices for a half-dozen count.

5. **When the popup appears for [range_lookup] select FALSE.**
   a. **If you don't see the drop-down you can just type 'false'.**

6. **Add a closing parenthesis.**

Your formula should look like the one shown below: Notice there are no spaces.

11	Question: What is the price of a half dozen Macaroons?			
12				
13	Macaroons	=VLOOKUP(A13,A2:D9,3,FALSE)		

7. **Hit Return/Enter.**

Your table should look like the one below.

	A	B	C	D
1	Pastry	Single	Half Dozen	Full Dozen
2	Glazed Donuts	$ 1.50	$ 7.50	$ 15.00
3	Buttermilk Donuts	$ 1.75	$ 9.00	$ 18.00
4	Jelly Donuts	$ 2.00	$ 10.50	$ 21.00
5	Bear Claws	$ 2.50	$ 13.50	$ 27.00
6	Cherry Tarts	$ 3.50	$ 19.50	$ 39.00
7	Macaroons	$ 2.50	$ 13.50	$ 27.00
8	Chocolate Eclairs	$ 3.00	$ 16.50	$ 33.00
9	Wedding cookies	$ 1.00	$ 6.00	$ 12.00
10				
11	Question: What is the price of a half dozen Macaroons?			
12				
13	Macaroons	$ 13.50		
14				

If you get the error message #NA, click into the formula cell (B13) and look at the formula bar. See if you have typed the formula exactly as shown, and with no spaces.

Once you get it right, try looking up different kinds of pastries and amounts to get a feel for the tool. This will help you memorize the steps to fill in the formula.

So, what's going on?

VLookup is a search tool that helps you find specific information within a large table of data. You tell VLookup the thing you are referencing. Then you tell VLookup the range of cells you want searched, and the table's column that has the data you're looking for.

The final argument is how you tell Excel whether you want an exact match or an approximate match. Since you want an exact match, you type FALSE.

Troubleshooting Errors in VLookup Results

You can pose multiple questions for a single VLookup task. But when you do, the likelihood of getting errors increases. In the next exercise, we will look up four items on the menu and then add them up for a total.

For this part of the exercise, we're going to intentionally introduce errors. This will help you troubleshoot your work if errors should happen on the job, which they often do.

1. **Delete text in row 11 and write "Question: Price of this pastry order for ½ dozen ea?"**
2. **Delete the contents of cells A13 and B13. Then write the following list.**
   b. **Cell A13**

      Jelly Donuts

   c. **Cell A14**

      Glazed Donuts

   d. **Cell A15**

      Cherry Tarts

   e. **Cell A16**

      Wedding Cookies
3. **Now go back to cell A15 and put one space after the 's' on 'Cherry Tarts'.**
4. **Return to cell A16 and misspell Cookies by replacing lowercase 'i' with 'l' (lowercase L).**
5. **Select cell B13 to start your VLookup formula.**

You will write the formula for Jelly Donuts in cell B13, and then drag the formula down three more cells to include the other pastries.

1. **Type =VL into cell B13 and then select VLOOKUP from the popup.**
2. **Click on Jelly Donuts in cell A13 then type a comma.**
3. **Select the table range from A2 through D9. It will appear as A2:D9. Follow with a comma.**

4. Type the numeral 3 into the formula followed by a comma.

Remember, the numeral 3 represents the table's 3rd column, which is the price for a half-dozen pastries.

5. Select FALSE from the popup (or type it in) and add a closed parenthesis.

Your formula should look like the one circled in the screenshot below.

	A	B	C	D
1	Pastry	Single	Half Dozen	Full Dozen
2	Glazed Donuts	$ 1.50	$ 7.50	$ 15.00
3	Buttermilk Donuts	$ 1.75	$ 9.00	$ 18.00
4	Jelly Donuts	$ 2.00	$ 10.50	$ 21.00
5	Bear Claws	$ 2.50	$ 13.50	$ 27.00
6	Cherry Tarts	$ 3.50	$ 19.50	$ 39.00
7	Macaroons	$ 2.50	$ 13.50	$ 27.00
8	Chocolate Eclairs	$ 3.00	$ 16.50	$ 33.00
9	Wedding cookies	$ 1.00	$ 6.00	$ 12.00
10				
11	Question: Price of this pastry order for 1/2 dozen ea?			
12				
13	Jelly Donuts	=VLOOKUP(A13,A2:D9,3,FALSE)		
14	Glazed Donuts			
15	Cherry Tarts			
16	Wedding Cookies			

6. Now hit Return/Enter.

The output should be 10.5. (See screenshot on facing page above)

7. With your cell pointer still on cell B13, copy it down three more cells alongside the remaining pastries.

8. Reminder: Hover your cursor over the tiny square on the bottom right corner of the cell pointer. When it turns into a black plus sign, click and hold the plus sign, and then drag it down three more cells.

This action should produce three #N/A errors as shown below.

	A	B	C	D
11	Question: Price of this pastry order for 1/2 dozen ea?			
12				
13	Jelly Donuts	$ 10.50		
14	Glazed Donuts	#N/A		
15	Cherry Tarts	#N/A		
16	Wedding Cookles	#N/A		

Let's talk about the first error for Glazed Donuts.

When you look at the pastry items in the table below, you'll notice that 'Glazed Donuts' is listed *above* 'Jelly Donuts'.

On the other hand, in the list of pastries that form the lookup_values of the VLookup formula (screenshot above), 'Glazed Donuts' is listed *below* 'Jelly Donuts'.

Because of this, when VLookup locates the position of 'Jelly Donuts' in the table array, it perceives 'Jelly Donuts' as the top of this list as well.

So VLookup shifts the number of rows of the table array downwards, from A2:D9 to A4:D11, such that row 4, where 'Jelly Donuts' is listed, winds up on top. For this reason, VLookup can no longer "see" row 2, where 'Glazed Donuts' is located, so it outputs #N/A.

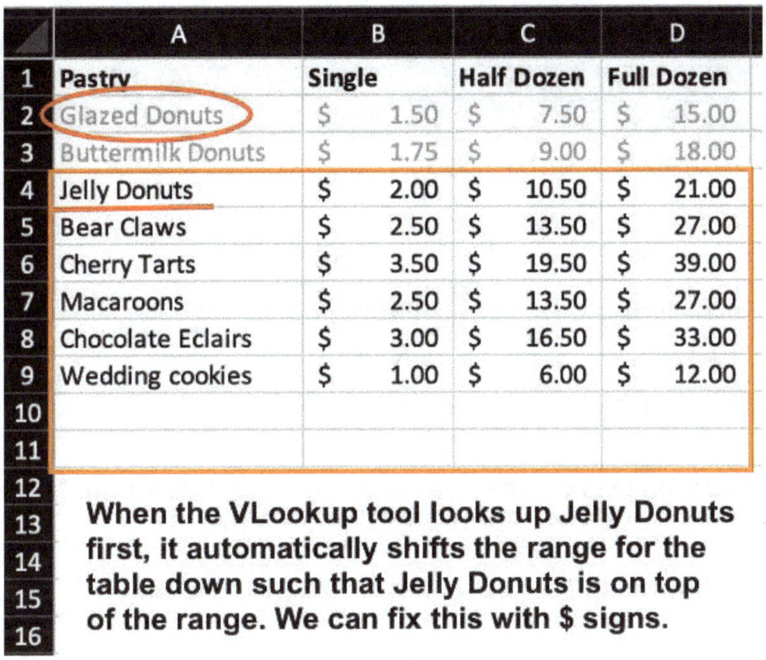

	A	B		C		D	
1	Pastry	Single		Half Dozen		Full Dozen	
2	Glazed Donuts	$	1.50	$	7.50	$	15.00
3	Buttermilk Donuts	$	1.75	$	9.00	$	18.00
4	Jelly Donuts	$	2.00	$	10.50	$	21.00
5	Bear Claws	$	2.50	$	13.50	$	27.00
6	Cherry Tarts	$	3.50	$	19.50	$	39.00
7	Macaroons	$	2.50	$	13.50	$	27.00
8	Chocolate Eclairs	$	3.00	$	16.50	$	33.00
9	Wedding cookies	$	1.00	$	6.00	$	12.00
10							
11							
12							
13							
14							
15							
16							

In *Project 5 Amortization Table*, you learned that when a formula that refers to values from other cells is copied and pasted, the formula adjusts its references *relative* to the new location. This is known as a *relative reference*.

What you need is a way to turn a relative reference into a fixed range of cells, which Excel calls *absolute reference.*

Let's apply *absolute reference* to this part of the project.

Create Absolute Reference for Table Array

Here's how to change a relative reference to an absolute reference.

1. Select the cell for the VLookup formula, cell B13, and look at the formula for the table array in the Formula Bar; A2:D9.

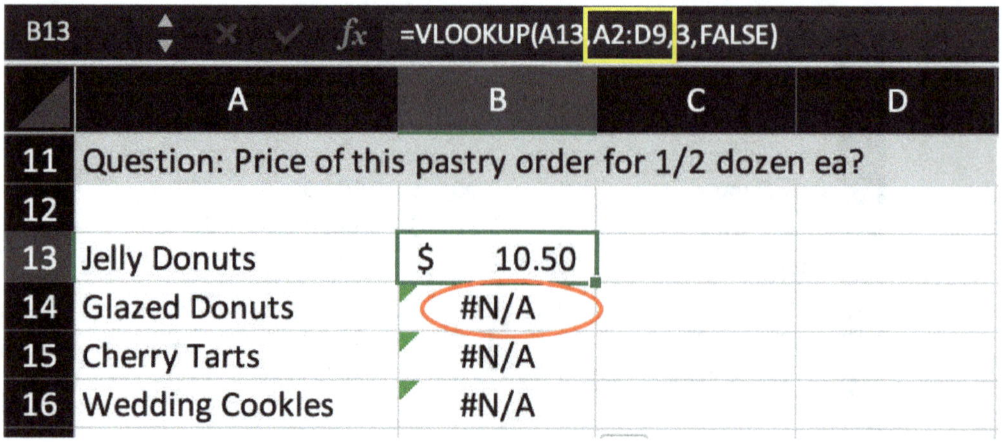

2. **Add a dollar sign ($) before each letter and number so the table array formula looks like this: (VLOOKUP,A15,$A$2:$D$9,3,FALSE).**

3. **Hit Return/Enter.**

4. **Delete all of the #N/As in Cells B16, 17, and 18.**

5. **Click back into cell B15 and copy the formula down three cells.**

Now you should see the price for the Glazed Donuts.

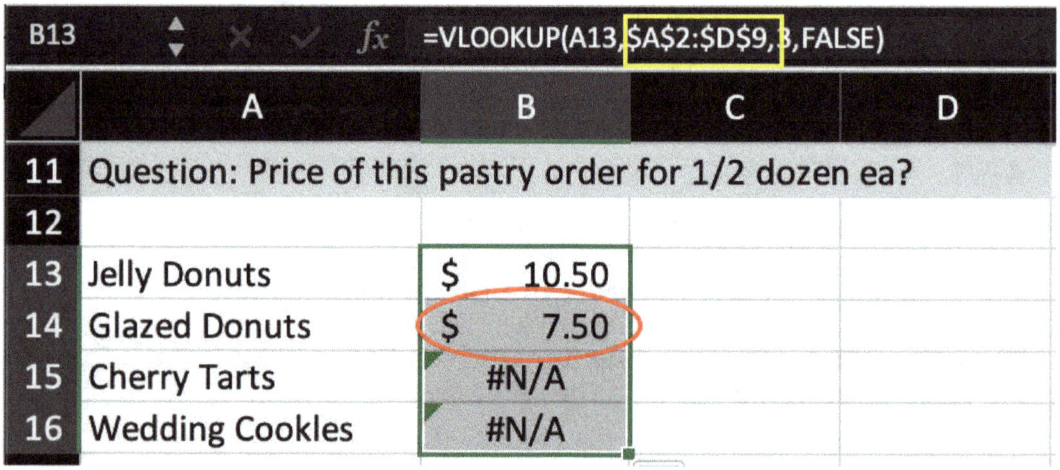

That problem is solved. Now we need to troubleshoot the other two errors. Recall when we filled out this list, we added an extra space after "Cherry Tarts" and we deliberately misspelled "Wedding Cookles".

6. **Return to cell A15 and delete the space at the end of "Cherry Tarts" and hit RETURN on Mac, ENTER on Windows.**

7. **Return to cell A16 and spell "Cookies" correctly and hit RETURN/ENTER.**

	A	B	C	D
11	Question: Price of this pastry order for 1/2 dozen ea?			
12				
13	Jelly Donuts	$ 10.50		
14	Glazed Donuts	$ 7.50		
15	Cherry Tarts	$ 19.50		
16	Wedding Cookies	$ 6.00		
17	**Total**	**$ 43.50**		

The cells should automatically correct and look like the ones above.

To total up the charges:

8. **Add the word "Total" to cell A17.**
9. **Enter the following formula in cell B17:**

   =Sum(B13:B16)

If you happened to spell "cookies" in all lower case instead of using capital letters, it's ok, VLookup doesn't distinguish between upper case and lower case.

Now you know three common errors to look for or guard against when using the VLookup tool: *relative reference* **instead of** *absolute reference*, **spaces at the end of words, and misspellings.**

VLookup: Compiling Information From Multiple Tables

In this exercise, we will complete a VLookup Revenue Table called the 'Vitamin & Supplement Table' by filling in two columns, one for the product category and one for the region where the products were sold.

On the *Excel In A Snap Project Worksheets* file, select the 8. VLookup Revenue Table worksheet.

If you don't have that file, you can fill in your own using the screenshot on the next page as a guide.

These two tables are the source material for the main table shown on the 8. VLookup Product & Sales worksheet.

Product Table

Product Name	Category
Protein Shake	Supplements
Ginseng Shot	Supplements
Multivitamin Pack	Supplements
Omega-3 Capsules	Supplements
Vegan Protein Powder	Health Foods
Collagen Powder	Health Foods
Organic Green Tea	Beverages
Chia Seed Snack	Health Foods
Energy Bar	Snacks
Spirulina Tablets	Supplements
Herbal Tea Mix	Beverages
Almond Butter	Health Foods

Salesperson Table

Salesperson	Manager	Plan	Region
John Baker	Karen Wilson	Gold	West
Samantha Lee	Karen Wilson	Platinum	East
Maria Gonzalez	Michael Brooks	Silver	North
James Carter	Michael Brooks	Gold	South
Linda Nguyen	Sophia Clark	Platinum	West
Alex Smith	Sophia Clark	Silver	East
Betty Johnson	Karen Wilson	Gold	North
Daniel Kim	Michael Brooks	Platinum	South

The data we use to fill the Product Category and Rep's Region columns (shown on next page) will be drawn from the two tables on the VLookup Product & Sales sheet (shown above).

If you want to construct your own Vitamin & Supplement Revenues table, create a new sheet, by clicking the '+' symbol at the bottom of the Excel screen. Double click the tab to name it '8. VLookup Revenue Table'.

Tip: The 'Vitamin and Supplement Table' heading on the table below is a text box, similar to the one we made for the Amortization Table in Project 5. That's how you can have a centered title above categories for each column, all in row 1.

It's a good idea to keep the category labels on row one. A lower category row might confuse the VLookup tool.

Text Box Reminder: **Click the Insert tab on the Excel menu bar, then click the down arrow on the Text toolbox, look to the right for the tilted blue capital 'A' symbol. Click on the Text Box symbol (square white-lined paper symbol). When the textbox icon appears on the screen, use your mouse or touchpad to navigate it to the header row and fill it in with the title.**

Before you enter the dollar figures in column D, select the column and format it for dollar signs. With the Home tab selected, click the dollar sign symbol [$] in the number formatting section on the ribbon.

Once the Vitamin & Supplement Table is complete, the VP of sales will be able to sort the revenue column from highest to lowest to see which salespeople and products are generating the most revenue and in which regions, among other things. Let's get started.

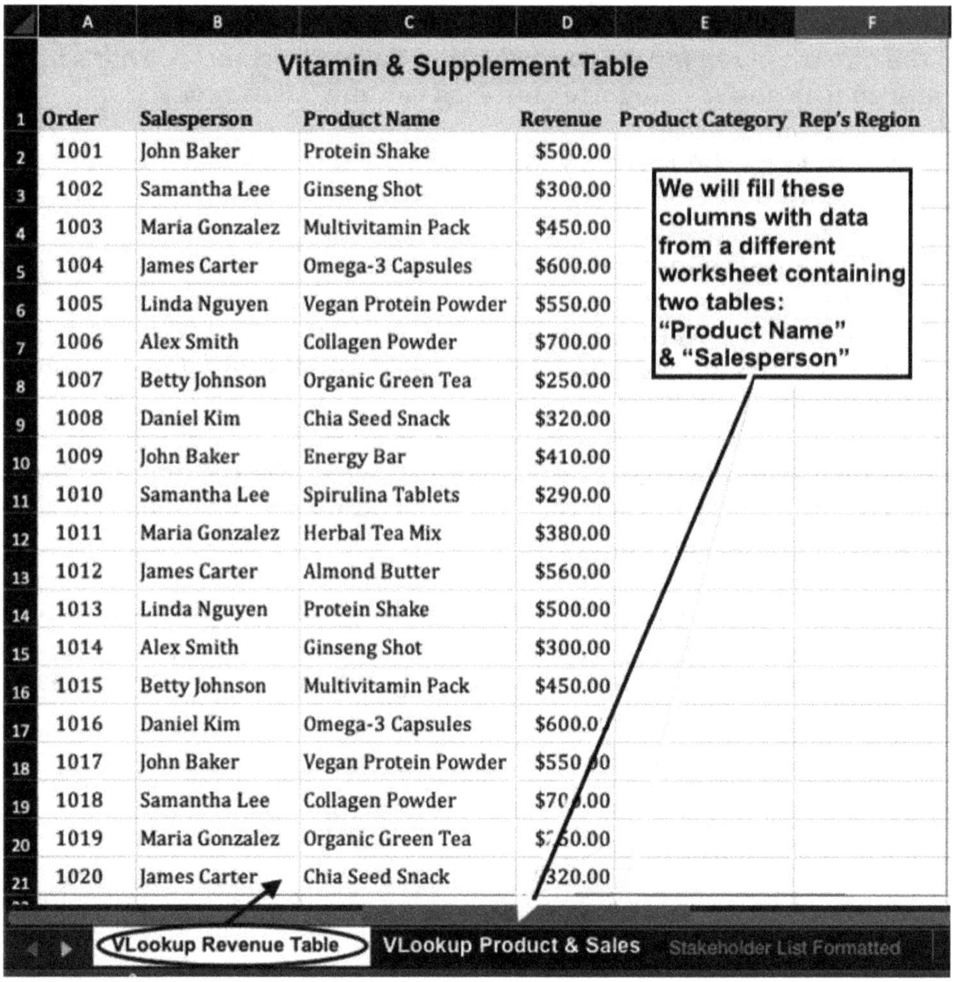

Order	Salesperson	Product Name	Revenue	Product Category	Rep's Region
1001	John Baker	Protein Shake	$500.00		
1002	Samantha Lee	Ginseng Shot	$300.00		
1003	Maria Gonzalez	Multivitamin Pack	$450.00		
1004	James Carter	Omega-3 Capsules	$600.00		
1005	Linda Nguyen	Vegan Protein Powder	$550.00		
1006	Alex Smith	Collagen Powder	$700.00		
1007	Betty Johnson	Organic Green Tea	$250.00		
1008	Daniel Kim	Chia Seed Snack	$320.00		
1009	John Baker	Energy Bar	$410.00		
1010	Samantha Lee	Spirulina Tablets	$290.00		
1011	Maria Gonzalez	Herbal Tea Mix	$380.00		
1012	James Carter	Almond Butter	$560.00		
1013	Linda Nguyen	Protein Shake	$500.00		
1014	Alex Smith	Ginseng Shot	$300.00		
1015	Betty Johnson	Multivitamin Pack	$450.00		
1016	Daniel Kim	Omega-3 Capsules	$600.00		
1017	John Baker	Vegan Protein Powder	$550.00		
1018	Samantha Lee	Collagen Powder	$700.00		
1019	Maria Gonzalez	Organic Green Tea	$250.00		
1020	James Carter	Chia Seed Snack	$320.00		

Referencing Tables on Another Worksheet With VLookup

1. **On the Vitamin & Supplement Table (see facing page on the left) select cell E2, under the heading "Product Category" and enter =VLOOKUP.**

2. **Then click on 'Protein Shake' in cell C2 and add a comma.**

Now we're going to switch over to the Product & Salesperson worksheet.

3. **Go to the bottom of the Excel window and click on the tab VLookup Product & Sales.**

4. **On the left-hand table select all the data beneath the headers: Cells B3 through C14 (or B3:C14).**

5. **To add the Absolute Reference, hit □ T on Mac, or Function F4 on Windows (or add in the $ signs manually) and add a comma.**

Notice that the Category column (screenshot on right) is in column C of the worksheet, but it's the 2nd column of the table.

This is one of those cases where the column of the referenced data on the table does not correspond to the column of the worksheet.

The VLookup tool will only count the columns in your table_array, i.e., your selection.

We will stay on this sheet until the VLookup formula is complete, at which point the tool will automatically take us back to the original table on the prior sheet.

	A	B	C
1			
2		**Product Name**	**Category**
3		Protein Shake	Supplements
4		Ginseng Shot	Supplements
5		Multivitamin Pack	Supplements
6		Omega-3 Capsules	Supplements
7		Vegan Protein Powder	Health Foods
8		Collagen Powder	Health Foods
9		Organic Green Tea	Beverages
10		Chia Seed Snack	Health Foods
11		Energy Bar	Snacks
12		Spirulina Tablets	Supplements
13		Herbal Tea Mix	Beverages
14		Almond Butter	Health Foods

6. **Type in 2 (meaning you want the value in the 2nd column of the selection, which is C3), add a comma, then FALSE, followed by closed parenthesis but don't hit Return/Enter yet.**

Here is what your VLookup formula should look like once it's done.

```
fx  =VLOOKUP(C2,'Vlookup Product & Sales'!$B$3:$C$14,2,FALSE)
```

Notice that in the VLookup formula, the text after 'C2,' is the argument for the table array which begins with the name of the worksheet from which the data is drawn, 'VLookup Product & Sales' followed by !, and then the coordinates for the range of cells that make up the table array. This part of the argument shows the name of the worksheet from which the data was drawn.

Once the formula is filled out, and you hit Return/Enter, the VLookup tool will take you back to the worksheet with the formula. In the cell where the formula was entered (E2), the formula's output "Supplements" will be displayed.

7. **Select cell E2, hover your pointer over the bottom right corner until it turns to a plus sign, then double-click to copy the cell's formula to the bottom of the table.**

When you're done, the column should fill in as depicted in the screenshot on the facing page.

E2 =VLOOKUP(C2,'Product & Salesperson'!$B$3:$C$14,2,FALSE)

	A	B	C	D	E	F	G	H
1	Order	Salesperson	Product Name	Revenue	Product Category	Rep's Region		
2	1001	John Baker	Protein Shake	$500.00	Supplements			
3	1002	Samantha Lee	Ginseng Shot	$300.00	Supplements			
4	1003	Maria Gonzalez	Multivitamin Pack	$450.00	Supplements			
5	1004	James Carter	Omega-3 Capsules	$600.00	Supplements			
6	1005	Linda Nguyen	Vegan Protein Powder	$550.00	Health Foods			
7	1006	Alex Smith	Collagen Powder	$700.00	Health Foods			
8	1007	Betty Johnson	Organic Green Tea	$250.00	Beverages			
9	1008	Daniel Kim	Chia Seed Snack	$320.00	Health Foods			
10	1009	John Baker	Energy Bar	$410.00	Snacks			
11	1010	Samantha Lee	Spirulina Tablets	$290.00	Supplements			
12	1011	Maria Gonzalez	Herbal Tea Mix	$380.00	Beverages			
13	1012	James Carter	Almond Butter	$560.00	Health Foods			
14	1013	Linda Nguyen	Protein Shake	$500.00	Supplements			
15	1014	Alex Smith	Ginseng Shot	$300.00	Supplements			
16	1015	Betty Johnson	Multivitamin Pack	$450.00	Supplements			
17	1016	Daniel Kim	Omega-3 Capsules	$600.00	Supplements			
18	1017	John Baker	Vegan Protein Powder	$550.00	Health Foods			
19	1018	Samantha Lee	Collagen Powder	$700.00	Health Foods			
20	1019	Maria Gonzalez	Organic Green Tea	$250.00	Beverages			
21	1020	James Carter	Chia Seed Snack	$320.00	Health Foods			

Now let's repeat the process to fill in the salespersons' regions in column F. But this time, for the [range_lookup] field, we will choose TRUE.

Remember, TRUE is the default value for this argument and would be used if the argument was blank.

The advantage of choosing TRUE is that the VLookup tool will ignore minor spelling errors or extra spaces. However, if you don't alphabetize both lists before choosing TRUE you are likely to get a lot of errors.

We will do it wrong first, and then do it right so you can see the importance of preparing both tables.

8. **Return to the Vitamin & Supplements Table on the <u>VLookup Revenue Table</u> worksheet (see facing page) place your pointer in cell F2 (just beneath <u>Rep's Region</u>) and begin the formula =VLookup.**

9. **Click on the name "John Baker" in cell B2 and add a comma.**

10. **Go to the VLookup <u>Product & Sales</u> worksheet and on the table to the right (Salesperson Table) select all the data: Cells E3 through H10. Remember to hit □ T on Mac, or Function F4 on Windows to create an absolute reference to your source data, and then add a comma.**

Once you've selected the table range, you will see a small black rectangle on the lower right beneath the table displaying the alphanumeric range of '8R x 4C' (see screenshot below). This tells us that the table range has 8 rows and 4 columns. We are looking for data in the <u>Region</u> column, which is column 4.

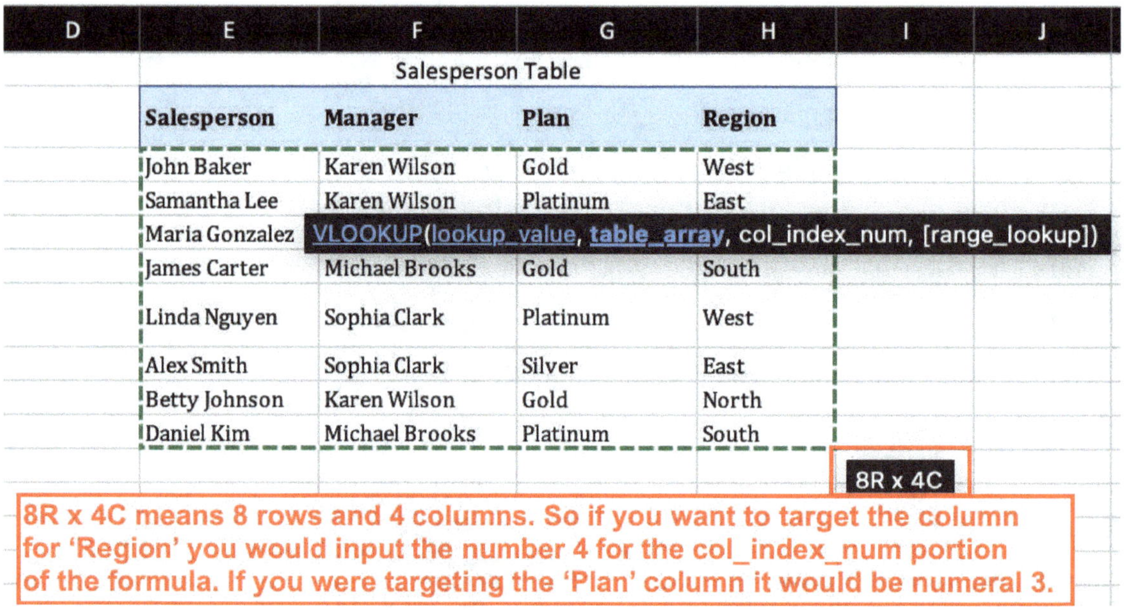

11. **Type in 4 (to reference, the 4th column of the Salesperson Table), followed by a comma, type TRUE, a close parenthesis, and then hit RETURN/ENTER.**

Once again you will be taken back to the worksheet where the formula was entered.

12. **Select cell F2 (the word 'South') and copy the cell down to the bottom of the table.**

The results should look like the following table.

	A	B	C	D	E	F
	Vitamin & Supplement Table					
1	**Order**	**Salesperson**	**Product Name**	**Revenue**	**Product Category**	**Rep's Region**
2	1001	John Baker	Protein Shake	$500.00	Supplements	South
3	1002	Samantha Lee	Ginseng Shot	$300.00	Supplements	South
4	1003	Maria Gonzalez	Multivitamin Pack	$450.00	Supplements	South
5	1004	James Carter	Omega-3 Capsules	$600.00	Supplements	South
6	1005	Linda Nguyen	Vegan Protein Powder	$550.00	Health Foods	South
7	1006	Alex Smith	Collagen Powder	$700.00	Health Foods	#N/A
8	1007	Betty Johnson	Organic Green Tea	$250.00	Beverages	#N/A
9	1008	Daniel Kim	Chia Seed Snack	$320.00	Health Foods	#N/A
10	1009	John Baker	Energy Bar	$410.00	Snacks	South
11	1010	Samantha Lee	Spirulina Tablets	$290.00	Supplements	South
12	1011	Maria Gonzalez	Herbal Tea Mix	$380.00	Beverages	South
13	1012	James Carter	Almond Butter	$560.00	Health Foods	South
14	1013	Linda Nguyen	Protein Shake	$500.00	Supplements	South
15	1014	Alex Smith	Ginseng Shot	$300.00	Supplements	#N/A
16	1015	Betty Johnson	Multivitamin Pack	$450.00	Supplements	#N/A
17	1016	Daniel Kim	Omega-3 Capsules	$600.00	Supplements	#N/A
18	1017	John Baker	Vegan Protein Powder	$550.00	Health Foods	South
19	1018	Samantha Lee	Collagen Powder	$700.00	Health Foods	South
20	1019	Maria Gonzalez	Organic Green Tea	$250.00	Beverages	South
21	1020	James Carter	Chia Seed Snack	$320.00	Health Foods	South

The error codes you see above are the likely result when you enter TRUE in your [range_lookup] field without first putting both columns in alphabetical order.

Let's do that now.

Alphabetizing Data

1. **On the <u>Vitamin & Supplements Table</u>, select cell B1 (Salesperson).**

2. **Click the <u>Data</u> tab in the Excel menu (screenshot below on left), and then in the <u>Sort & Filter</u> section of the ribbon, click the Filter Symbol to insert "down" arrows next to each of the column labels.**

3. **Click the down-arrow next to 'Salesperson' in cell B1 and in the drop-down below <u>Sort</u>, click <u>Ascending (see screenshot below on right)</u>.**

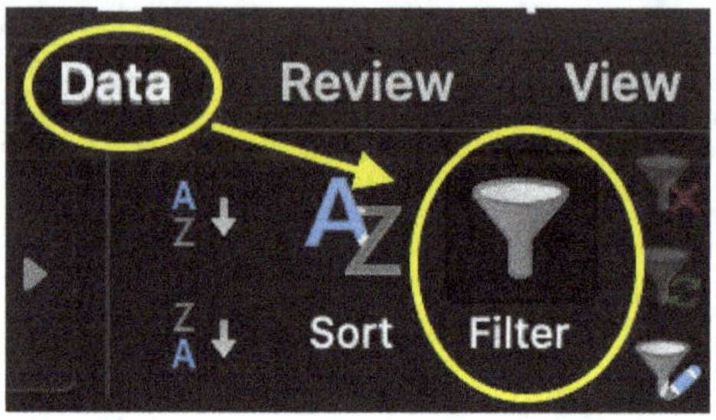

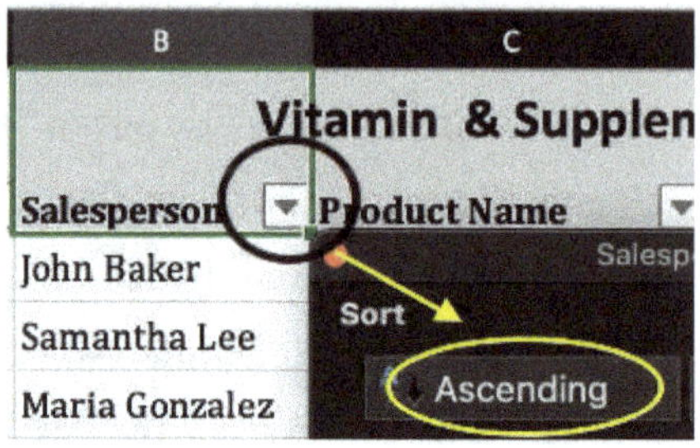

4. **Return to the <u>VLookup Product & Sales</u> worksheet tab, and in the <u>Salesperson</u> table create filters for each of the column names and then alphabetize the <u>Region</u> column in ascending order.**

The resulting columns should look like the ones below.

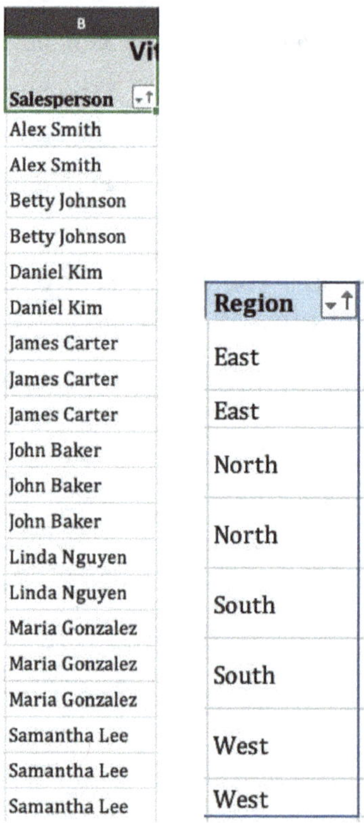

Referencing the Alphabetized Data

1. Return to the Vitamin & Supplements Table located in the VLookup Revenue Table worksheet tab, and erase everything in Column F below the Reps Region column name. Be careful not to delete the contents of the cell F1 Reps Region.

2. Place your pointer in cell F2 (just beneath Rep's Region) and begin typing the formula =VLookup.

3. Click on the name "Alex Smith" in cell B2, and add a comma.

4. Go to the VLookup Product & Salesperson worksheet tab and on the Salesperson Table, select all the data: Cells E3 through H10. Remember to hit T on Mac, or Function F4 on Windows, to create an absolute reference for your table array.

5. Type a comma, followed by the number 4 to reference the 4th column of the Salesperson Table, followed by one more comma. Then type TRUE followed by a close parenthesis, and hit RETURN/ENTER.

Once again you will be taken back to the worksheet with the formula.

6. Select cell F2 (the word 'East') and copy the cell down to the bottom of the table.

When you're done, the table should like the one below.

If you would like to return the table to its original order, you can sort Column A.

F2 =VLOOKUP(B2,'Vlookup Product & Sales'!$E$3:$H$10,4,TRUE)

Vitamin & Supplement Table

Order	Salesperson	Product Name	Revenu	Product Catego	Rep's Region
1006	Alex Smith	Collagen Powder	$700.00	Health Foods	East
1014	Alex Smith	Ginseng Shot	$300.00	Supplements	East
1007	Betty Johnson	Organic Green Tea	$250.00	Beverages	North
1015	Betty Johnson	Multivitamin Pack	$450.00	Supplements	North
1008	Daniel Kim	Chia Seed Snack	$320.00	Health Foods	South
1016	Daniel Kim	Omega-3 Capsules	$600.00	Supplements	South
1004	James Carter	Omega-3 Capsules	$600.00	Supplements	South
1012	James Carter	Almond Butter	$560.00	Health Foods	South
1020	James Carter	Chia Seed Snack	$320.00	Health Foods	South
1001	John Baker	Protein Shake	$500.00	Supplements	West
1009	John Baker	Energy Bar	$410.00	Snacks	West
1017	John Baker	Vegan Protein Powder	$550.00	Health Foods	West
1005	Linda Nguyen	Vegan Protein Powder	$550.00	Health Foods	West
1013	Linda Nguyen	Protein Shake	$500.00	Supplements	West
1003	Maria Gonzalez	Multivitamin Pack	$450.00	Supplements	West
1011	Maria Gonzalez	Herbal Tea Mix	$380.00	Beverages	West
1019	Maria Gonzalez	Organic Green Tea	$250.00	Beverages	West
1002	Samantha Lee	Ginseng Shot	$300.00	Supplements	West
1010	Samantha Lee	Spirulina Tablets	$290.00	Supplements	West
1018	Samantha Lee	Collagen Powder	$700.00	Health Foods	West

Final Thoughts On VLookup

Keep in mind that when you use VLookup, you should always create an *absolute reference* **to the range of the cells you selected, inserting $ both before the column letters and row numbers.**

When you choose FALSE for your *range_lookup*, **minor spelling errors or extra spaces can cause errors. If you use the argument TRUE instead, the VLookup search function will be more forgiving of minor errors, but you must also alphabetize both the column that contains the lookup value, and the column specified by the column index number to avoid errors.**

Feel free to use these tables as a sandbox and explore various VLookup scenarios. The more you practice, the more comfortable you will become with this complicated but crucial data retrieval tool.

And there you have it! You've just learned another of Excel's advanced features. Congratulations!

One More Thing Before You Go

While this workbook does not contain absolutely everything there is to know about Excel, if you can master the exercises and projects in this book, not only should you be fine in most jobs that require fluency in Excel, but you could also probably become your office's Excel go-to person.

If your job requires additional Excel expertise, finding tutorials online that bring you up to speed shouldn't be any trouble once you know the basics.

It's a good idea to keep this volume nearby while you are using Excel in case you need a reminder on how to execute various tasks. You can either refer to the Table of Contents at the front of the book, or the index at the back.

Leave a Quick Review

If you felt this tutorial was helpful and would like to share that with the public, please go to my website: www.INaSnapGuides.com and click on the hot button that says "Leave a Review". It will take you directly to my Amazon page where you can leave a quick review.

So, happy Excelling!

INDEX

Index

Index

www.ingramcontent.com/pod-product-compliance
Lightning Source LLC
LaVergne TN
LVHW082344200926
848481LV00012B/3450